 Portions of this were previously published in The Periphery and Belt Magazine.

First Printing, 2015

ISBN: 9 780996 836708

Belt Publishing
http://www.beltmag.com

Book design, cover design, and illustrations by Haley Suzanne Stone

# *How to* LIVE IN DETROIT WITHOUT BEING A JACKASS

By Aaron Foley

# TABLE OF CONTENTS

# INTRODUCTION

We're living in a time when everyone thinks they're an expert on Detroit.

Everyone is an urban planner. Everyone knows what's best for Detroit, no matter how long they've lived here. Everyone's a scholar, everyone knows the real deal, everyone's a problem solver.

But no one can ever be an expert on Detroit. The city is just too large for anyone to do a comprehensive analysis of life in this city. There are historical chronicles, guidebooks, and almanacs of Detroit; there are collections of essays; there are stories, both fiction and non. But it is impossible to capture the Detroit experience in one place.

So that's my disclaimer. This book is by no means comprehensive or cumulative. But I'll be confident enough to say that it should be a starter. A warm-up. A little bit of light in the darkness.

Now if you're reading this and already proclaim yourself an expert on Detroit, stop right now. If you've got a stack of local history books sitting on your kitchen counter, if you're at the ready on every online forum with someone asking a question about Detroit, if you mainline melted wax from Motown LPs and your piss is Faygo Redpop, this book is not for you.

But if you're ready to learn something new about Detroit, read on. Because we're all learning something new about Detroit, even us so-called experts. But I didn't want to write a book about things you can easily Google. If you want a book about famous people from Detroit, go read the Wikipedia list of famous people from Detroit. If you want to know where the best restaurants are, go to Yelp or somewhere.

It is an interesting time to be in Detroit, though. Writing this was a challenge, because every time I stated something declarative about a particular subject, an announcement came down saying it had changed. Things are changing rapidly here, and it's difficult to keep up.

For many of us, Detroit is changing too fast. We are losing, very quickly, people and places that we have known all our lives. And it seems sometimes like Detroit's newer residents are all too quick to say good riddance to things that are sentimental to old-timers.

That's where the "jackass" part comes in. A lot of what I have written deals in the history of Detroit, and how we learn from our past. But again, Detroit is so large, so diverse, that one person's past is certainly not the next's. So I'm just offering what I know, the stories I've been told, the lessons I've learned, in the hope that you will connect Detroit's history to its future, and not be a dick about it.

It's a little hard living here sometimes. But it's easy not to be a jackass. Here's how.

*I am from Detroit.*

**MOTOWN!**

—Big Brother Almighty, *School Daze*

# CHAPTER 1

## SEVEN RULES FOR LIVING IN DETROIT: OR, HOW TO NOT LOOK LIKE A DUMBASS THE MOMENT YOU GET HERE

Let's begin with some rules for how to live in Detroit. The first one is to remember that a coney dog, the famous Detroit delicacy, does not define the city. It is just a hot dog with meat sauce on it.

I don't want to say that the coney dog is not special. It's just not spectacular, even if almost every list, travel piece, think piece, and essay about Detroit mentions it. It is simply cheap meat on top of cheaper meat with cheap garnish.

The coney dog has earned its rightful place, but it is so deeply ingrained in Detroit culture that newcomers and visitors—I won't say outsiders—begin to associate this city with coney dogs alone. "Oh, I've gotta get a coney!" "Where are those coney places?" "What's the best coney?"

Our two most famous coney dog spots are American Coney Island and Lafayette Coney Island, and they both have the good fortune of being located in downtown Detroit. They seat few, and they only take cash. They are iconic, legendary restaurants—but they are not the only way to define this city. The other icons of Detroit culture—the plant where Henry Ford instituted the $5-a-day wage, the two studios where Berry Gordy made music to make the world dance, and the new farms reclaiming the earth where ribbon farms of the 1800s were plentiful—are perhaps more important.

Eating a coney dog does not define living in Detroit, because living here is not simple. It can be hard to live here, but easy existence is boring. Here in Detroit, you *live*. You live experiences unmatched.

Detroit is much more than restaurants; it is the churches, the ubiquitous, required soul music, the children, the sports, the cars, the schools, the endless line dances fashioned from creative minds, the art we could have lost and the love we find in the littlest things.

The second rule of living in Detroit is to recognize how large and diverse it is. No two experiences are shared. Knowing how many people—currently around 700,000 on a good day, down from highs of 2 million—inhabit its 139-square-mile space is key to going forward, because your Detroit experience will be different than anyone else's.

Don't trust the listicles and slideshows, no matter how inspiring and positive they may be. Much that has been written about Detroit and is still being written about Detroit is done by the hands of residents still getting their feet wet themselves.

That's a good segue into your third rule of living here: never, ever weigh your Detroit experience against the next person's. I've seen people come here after, like, a *year*, and all of a sudden are dictating to people who have lived here forever what it's like in Detroit. What arrogance.

For instance, I visited a trendy home-design store in the city where they sell these canvas tote bags that read: "I'm just more Detroit than you." How does carrying a tote bag make someone more Detroit than me? When I was in kindergarten, my mom and I spent a night sleeping in our bathtub because the guy in the apartment next door decided that was a good night to shoot his wife in a domestic dispute. I thought the blood on the walls of the hallway was ketchup. That's just one of the crazy stories a Detroiter might have. Put that on your tote bag.

Fourth rule: Be careful of people who make rules and tell you they are actually more Detroit than you. There are Detroiters all around who will try to tell you that there are certain authenticity tests you must pass before you can call yourself a Detroiter. Absolutely none of those tests will be accurate, because as I said before, we all have different experiences.

Some will try to say that you haven't lived in Detroit unless you've gone to this bar, or you haven't lived in Detroit unless you've had this crazy thing happen to you, or you don't really live in Detroit because you don't live in a certain neighborhood, or you're not really a Detroiter unless you've lived here for a certain amount of time, or you're not really Detroit unless you've met some other out-of-thin-air checklist most likely made up by some kid at Wayne State who thinks he knows every goddamn thing because he survived getting mugged outside the Temple Bar. It's all bullshit.

However, there is one thing you will be quizzed on. We introduce ourselves not just by saying hello, but asking where you went to high school. You see, in casual conversation, once two or more people find out they are both from Detroit, we like to know immediately if we have common ground. So we ask about high school. High school gives one clues as to the other's upbringing and background. We know where the east-side schools are and where the west-side schools are. And we don't judge your upbringing or background; we simply ask because most native Detroiters are separated by six degrees or less. Seriously! Everybody knows somebody who knows so-and-so. Yeah, someone's cousin's auntie used to be a hairdresser for Aretha Franklin or something. That's how it works, and that's how we make conversation.

If your high school is not in Detroit, then we might find out you're from the suburbs and then you *might* get judged. But we'll talk about that later.

The fifth rule applies to all you transplants from New York City and other places that are really expensive: please do not consider moving to Detroit part of a deep, soul-touching experience that will wash clean the sins of your past and renew your spiritual energy to live in your purpose. This ain't fucking *Eat, Pray, Love*, OK? You likely moved here because you either wanted to further your career or you got priced out of where you were. Please don't call yourself a "pioneer," because that implies you are settling—colonizing?—uninhabited land. People already live here. Don't say you're on "vacation"—does this look like a resort to you? Don't say you're on "safari," because here, safari is "Africa" and safari is "looking at things in the wild," and we're starting to unearth some nasty racial undertones, aren't we? And boy, we're going to talk about race a lot if you decide to keep reading.

(A special note for you millennials: If you are in your 20s and 30s and feel like you are "finding yourself" in Detroit, please realize that you are in your 20s and 30s and you'd be "finding yourself" no matter where you live. It's just coincidence that you're doing it here. Detroit didn't make you this way. Age and the wisdom that comes with it did.)

The sixth rule of Detroit is crucial: the sign says "McNichols" but it's called "Six Mile." Don't ask questions, just do it. Say Six Mile, Six Mile. It'll be McNichols on Google Maps and other apps, but Six Mile is what leaves your lips.

The final rule is simple: pay attention. Listen to people. Real people. Life in Detroit cannot be gleaned from an article, no matter how shareable on social media it seems. You have to absorb everything here in real time. It will not be easy, but do not put the blame on Detroit: life is an obstacle course no matter where you are. But people are paramount. Treat people with respect and dignity. Not just in Detroit, but especially in Detroit. It's pretty basic, but you'd be surprised how many people don't abide by this. And why's that? Because people get so wrapped up in things like coney dogs that they forget about humanity.

You are welcome in Detroit, but adjusting to living in Detroit will be complicated, and navigating it with ease will not come right away. Please don't expect it to. But when that moment comes when you've felt like you've got it all down pat, you'll know. Until that moment comes, however, join us in hoping that Detroit becomes a great place for not just the newcomers, but those of us that have been here. We can be curmudgeonly, because Detroit has been through hellish times. But deep down, we are hopeful. I am hopeful.

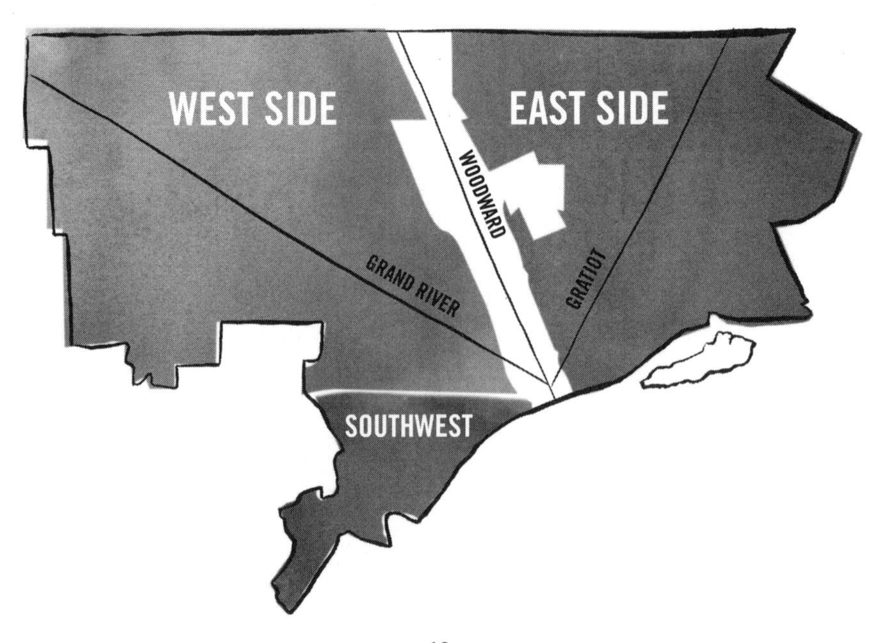

# READ THESE BOOKS BEFORE YOU GET ALL COMFY

- *Detroit: I Do Mind Dying: A Study in Urban Resolution*
  Dan Georgakas

- *Hard Stuff: The Autobiography of Mayor Coleman Young*
  Coleman Young and Lonnie Wheeler

- *Black Detroit and the Rise of the UAW*
  August Meier and Elliott M. Rudwick

- *The Detroit Almanac*
  Peter Gavrilovich and Bill McGraw

- *Detroit: An American Autopsy*
  Charlie LeDuff

- *Detroit: A Biography*
  Scott Martelle

- *Detroit City is the Place To Be: The Afterlife of an American Metropolis*
  Mark Binelli

- *The Origins of the Urban Crisis: Race and Inequality in Postwar Detroit*
  Thomas Sugrue

- *A Detroit Anthology*
  Anna Clark, ed.

*Welcome to the*

# MOTOR TOWN, BOOMIN' LIKE AN ATOM BOMB.

—Mayer Hawthorne, "A Long Time"

# CHAPTER 2

## THE QUICK-AND-DIRTY TOUR

These are the big places you should visit immediately upon moving here, if you haven't done so already. Many of these places are not within walking distance of each other, and none of them represent the whole of Detroit. But they are the city's most recognizable landmarks.

### EASTERN MARKET

Welcome to America's largest outdoor farmers' market, at its busiest on Saturday mornings. And because it's busy, please do *not* walk slowly or make dead stops in the middle of the aisles when you shop here! A comparable density of people can be found in the subways of New York City or Union Square in San Francisco. That said, the market itself is a must for first-timers, and quickly becomes a go-to the longer you live here. Farm-fresh produce and an array of butchers are the staples. Once a year is Flower Day, when farmers offer up the best of the best of their annuals and perennials on top of what is usually sold there. Aside from the farmers' market, the area is surrounded by bars, coffee shops, specialty markets, a few shops, and other businesses open during regular hours.

### DETROIT INSTITUTE OF ARTS

The DIA—and you're pronouncing that Dee-Eye-Aye, not dee-uh, the Spanish word for "day"—is not just the city's premier holder of art,

but one of the world's most-renowned art collections. Enough can't be said about the DIA; you will simply be lost in all that it has to offer. And while we're on the subject: none of the art was lost to the city's municipal bankruptcy filing. It is supported by not just Detroiters, but Southeast Michigan as a whole; residents in Wayne, Oakland, and Macomb counties approved a millage to give the museum additional funding. The DIA also serves as a popular event venue, as well as an occasional meeting spot thanks to stylish open spaces like Kresge Court.
*5200 Woodward Ave., Detroit, MI 48202*

## THE CHARLES H. WRIGHT MUSEUM OF AFRICAN-AMERICAN HISTORY

Here's a reminder that Detroit is the embodiment of modern black Americana. The Charles H. Wright is the country's largest black history museum, founded by a local legend who first envisioned a traveling black history exhibit. Do not think of it as the little brother of the DIA; both museums are equally important. The Charles H. Wright tracks the black American experience from the beginnings of slavery until the present, along with one-time-only exhibits and regular history lessons for all ages. It is also a popular event venue. (Black history aficionados should also make a point to visit Second Baptist Church in Greektown, which served as an Underground Railroad stop for runaway slaves making their way to Canada; the church occasionally allows visitors to see the hiding spot.)
*315 E. Warren Ave., Detroit, MI 48202*

## THE MOTOWN HISTORICAL MUSEUM

Museums, amirite? There's a big argument about how Detroit doesn't preserve its history because so much is being torn down, but it's curious that when you want to suggest some places for tourists to visit, museums always fall into the top suggestions. The Motown Museum, as it's more casually called, was founded by Esther Gordy Edwards, Motown Records founder Berry Gordy's older sister (and one-time executive at the company). As the story goes, Gordy Edwards was something of a pack rat, and held onto all of Motown's sheet music,

ticket stubs, programs, posters – any scrap of paper, any instrument or mixing board, anything that made Motown what it was. When Motown moved its headquarters to California, the original Studio A on West Grand Boulevard was retained and eventually became what's now the museum.
*2648 W. Grand Blvd., Detroit, MI 48208*

## MUSEUM OF CONTEMPORARY ART DETROIT

Every art-school grad with a DSLR and a CCW will hunt me down and murder me in the street if I fail to mention this place. No, but seriously—MOCAD is a fun place, and exactly what it is: A museum of contemporary art. It's far less fussy and ornate than the DIA or the Charles H. Wright, and is the template for every abandoned-space-turned-gallery in the city. Curiously, it's also rented out for huge events that don't quite gel with its aesthetic—like automaker parties during the North American International Auto Show, for instance—but that doesn't detract from it being a launching pad for local artists who have the honor of exhibiting there.
*4454 Woodward Ave., Detroit, MI 48201*

## DETROIT PEOPLE MOVER

You're either going to love it or you're not going to use it at all. A monorail with limited service that runs in a circle through downtown Detroit, the People Mover is popular on game days and during other big events. Art lovers should take special note of the works of art inside each of the 13 stations.

## BELLE ISLE

I guess you could say this is our Central Park, but I loathe that comparison. (A thing all Detroiters, not just me, hate: Comparing our landmarks to other cities' landmarks.) But there is a lot to offer on Belle Isle, an island in the Detroit River: a conservatory, a yacht club, a giant slide, a beach (that a lot of white people call Hipster Beach, but no one else has ever, ever called it that), a maritime museum, a nature zoo, an aquarium, a driving range, plenty of picnic and other outdoor space, a gorgeous fountain, trails, and so much more. It is owned by the city, but was recently leased to the state of Michigan's park system under a 30-year deal approved in 2013, and is officially being run as a state park. Depending on who you talk to, Belle Isle is also a wedding venue, a church picnic space, a racetrack, or a place for old-school classic cars to cruise. On a daily basis, it's fun to bike or walk there – and is accessible via public transportation. A state park pass is required to enter the park by car, and you'll want to drive slow if you do; an increase in patrolling recently has led to a crackdown on scofflaws.

## THE RENAISSANCE CENTER

So the thing about the RenCen is that if you've lived here for a long time, you're going to have a reason or a dozen to go here. It is the most recognizable skyscraper in the city's skyline. It is the headquarters of General Motors, but its construction in the 1970s was funded by Henry Ford's son. There is a hotel, some shops, restaurants, a movie theater (one of a handful in the city limits), and other event spaces. It's also architecturally uninteresting and confusing as hell to navigate on the inside. The RenCen is a sore spot for design snobs, and there's a bit of contention among city historians about whether the whole building was even worth the trouble of construction, but it's here and it ain't going away anytime soon. (The restaurants in the building *are* worth the trip, though.)

## DETROIT ATHLETIC CLUB

Holy shit, this place is expensive! It's a private, members-only club across the street from a courthouse; how much of a Detroit juxtaposition do you need? I'm only listing it because people who have not lived here very long start thinking about joining a gym, they see the name "Detroit Athletic Club," and they want to be so Detroit because it has Detroit in the name, and then balk when they discover that you not only to pay thousands of dollars in entrance fees, but thousands more in membership costs. That all said, the insides are gorgeous, and

if you're lucky enough to get a guest pass, take the day off and enjoy the Olympic-sized, Pewabic tile-lined swimming pool, top-notch equipment, and a good meal. It's an event space as well, but men must wear ties to be admitted.
*241 Madison Ave., Detroit, MI 48226*

## THE FISHER BUILDING

They call it Detroit's largest work of art, and with good reason. It is a skyscraper in Detroit's New Center neighborhood, a few miles outside downtown and notably across the street from the former headquarters of General Motors—a beautiful building in its own right. Back in the day, the Fisher coach-building family was contracted to build car bodies for GM. And, as automakers and their affiliates were basically shitting out cash and could build whatever they wanted, the Fishers spared no expense in creating their headquarters, commissioning architect Albert Kahn—who has designed several other notable buildings and homes in town—and several American and European artists to construct an art-deco masterpiece that includes vaulted ceilings adorned with gilded sculptures and paintings, and enough marble to piss off a mountain. A stroll through the first floor, now home to a number of shops and cafes, is unquestionably breathtaking.
*3011 W Grand Blvd., Detroit, MI 48202*

## THE GUARDIAN BUILDING

An orange-brick skyscraper, the Guardian is one of the most recognizable Detroit skyscrapers thanks not just to its art-deco exterior, but its gorgeous first-floor mural of the state of Michigan as well. Please visit this. Let everyone know you were here by posting it on social media. (No, seriously—the mural is beautiful; you won't be disappointed.)
*500 Griswold St., Detroit, MI 48226*

## THE PACKARD PLANT, THE HEIDELBERG PROJECT, AND MICHIGAN CENTRAL STATION

I feel obligated to mention this because these are the top three places

everyone looks for when visiting Detroit. Everyone wants to see the Packard Plant, the old auto factory with a famous bridge. Go see it soon, because the ruins that are there now have been purchased by a wealthy businessman and he has plans to... make them not look like ruins anymore. The Packard Plant is on the east side of Detroit and not too far from the Heidelberg Project, where Tyree Guyton has transformed vacant houses into eclectic artwork. (Not everyone in Detroit agrees that it's art, but if you don't think it's art, don't say it out loud in front of artsy Detroiters.) Go see that soon, too, because several of those structures are being lost to arson as I type. And then there's Michigan Central Station, the big, abandoned train station photographed in every single article about Detroit. (It's the massive rectangular building with no windows.) It's in Corktown, one of the city's more popular neighborhoods of late. But the station itself is closed off and, no, you can't go exploring inside—not legally, at least.
*Packard Plant, located at intersection of East Grand Boulevard and Concord Street; Heidelberg Project, 3600 Heidelberg St., Detroit, MI 48207 (and many surrounding addresses); Michigan Central Station, located in Corktown near the intersection of Michigan Avenue and 14th Street*

## GREEKTOWN

A German neighborhood that turned into a Greek neighborhood that doesn't have much Greek-ness at all anymore, except for the giant Greektown Casino and a few Greek restaurants. It is primarily an entertainment district; music plays from speakers while street artists quickly draw up caricatures of passers-by. It's always a destination for visitors because on top of the Greek restaurants—many of which are excellent—there are other top-notch places to eat. There are handfuls of Detroiters who think Greektown is pretty much Little Las Vegas in its cheesiness and kitsch, but the area's proximity to sports events as well as consistent preservation has made Greektown endure.

## MEXICANTOWN

What is Mexicantown, exactly? Some refer to Mexicantown as anywhere Mexicans live, so their definition is all of Southwest Detroit, where thousands of Mexicans live. Some refer to a broad area that's south of Corktown, adjacent to the Ambassador Bridge and extends into a few Southwest neighborhoods. And then there are those who refer specifically to a small collection of restaurants and bakeries. For these "you must go to this place now" purposes, I'm going with this third definition: Mexicantown is the area immediately off of Interstate 75 or the Ambassador Bridge to Canada, where some of the best Mexican restaurants—ranging from authentic to Americanized—are concentrated. Like Greektown, there are Detroiters who think the area is touristy, but it's a nice place to get your feet wet. (Note: you should not refer to all of Southwest Detroit as "Mexicantown," because immigrant groups from other Latin countries live across the area—as well as every other race and ethnicity, including a recent influx of Middle Eastern residents.)

---

The airport you'll likely use the most is Detroit Metropolitan Airport, which is not actually in Detroit—it's in a Wayne County suburb called Romulus, which is about a 20- or 30-minute drive from the city. (As with all airports, prepare for traffic getting there and long lines to board.) Other regional airports include City Airport (official name: Coleman A. Young International Airport), an airport on the city's east side that does not offer passenger service at the moment, and Oakland County International Airport to the north. You can also get out of town via Amtrak, Greyhound, and Megabus, all of which have stops in the city limits.

South Detroit is not real. It is a figment of Journey's imagination in the song "Don't Stop Believin'." There is Southwest Detroit, and there are places south of Detroit—that's called "Downriver." And there is Windsor in Canada, the only Canadian city that is technically south of the United States on a map. But no. Journey's Steve Perry told a magazine that "south Detroit" was solely good syntax for the mood of the song. Don't use this term, please. (Similarly, there is no "west Detroit" or "north Detroit." There was a city called East Detroit, but it rebranded itself as Eastpointe in the '90s.)

# LANDMARKS

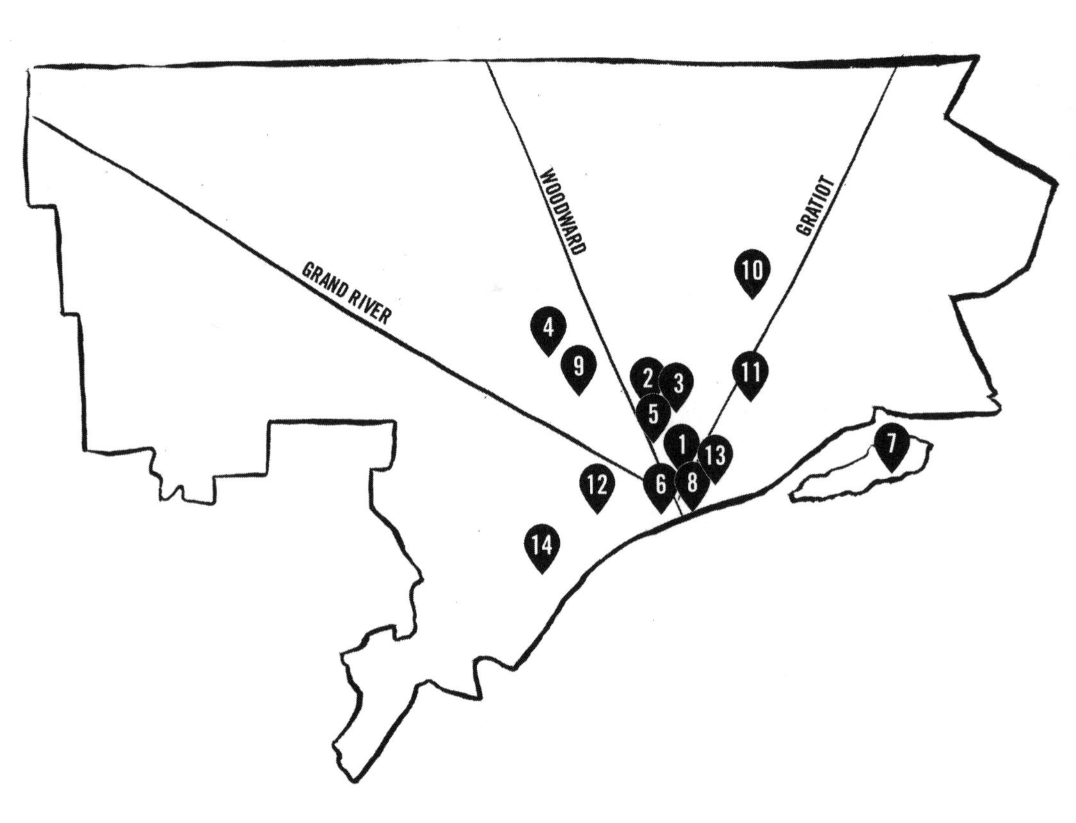


1. Eastern Market
2. Detroit Institute of Arts
3. The Charles H. Wright Museum of African-American History
4. The Motown Historical Museum
5. Museum of Contemorary Arts Detroit
6. The People Mover
7. Belle Isle
8. Notable Downtown Buildings: Renaissance Center, the Detroit Athletic Club, The Guardian Building
9. The Fisher Building
10. Packard Plant
11. The Heidelberg Project
12. Michigan Central Station
13. Greektown
14. Mexicantown

There are two small cities inside Detroit; their boundaries are surrounded by Detroit on all sides, yet they have separate governments and school systems from the city. They are Highland Park and Hamtramck.

**HIGHLAND PARK** once was a booming community that came of age as the automotive industry blossomed. Henry Ford built a Model T plant there, and Chrysler's world headquarters were once here. The industry's faltering in the 1980s dovetailed with the decade's crack epidemic (not to mention white flight and other woes that were plaguing Detroit before that decade), decimating the city from population highs of about 50,000 to just over 11,000 today. It is home, however, to a handful of streets that have preserved some of the finer Craftsman and other architecturally notable homes in the area.

**HAMTRAMCK** was one of the largest settlements for European immigrants, particularly the Poles who swarmed both this town and the Poletown neighborhood in Detroit, southeast of this city. A blue-collar, working man's town through and through, Hamtramck suffered a mighty blow when Chrysler closed the city's Dodge Plant in 1980. The last 20 years, however, have brought a large influx of Middle Eastern and South Asian immigrants, as well as continued immigration from Eastern European countries. The town's biggest demographics are Poles, Bangladeshis, and skinny white dudes who play in bands.

## THE BIG EVENTS

People often say Detroit is boring, but there's something going on every weekend. Here's the thing, though: There are so many events happening in and outside of the city that it's impossible to make an accurate list; some events are canceled, others sprout out of nowhere. The events that follow, however, are local traditions, and will probably give you a headache if you're trying to make your way through traffic.

# WINTER EVENTS

## NOEL NIGHT

A December holiday season event in Midtown, Noel Night draws thousands to Woodward Avenue around the DIA for winter-themed activities and a chance to shop the many area stores—as well as visit the DIA itself, and other cultural attractions in the area – after hours.

## THE "D" DROP

One of the newer local traditions, each night on New Year's Eve, a giant letter "D" lowers down above Campus Martius at midnight.

## NORTH AMERICAN INTERNATIONAL AUTO SHOW

In a nutshell, the "auto show" is an annual event held by the Detroit Auto Dealers Association for car companies to show what they will have in dealerships for the year. It's also an opportunity for car companies to show off new and future models to the automotive press across the world, making it one of the most well-attended car events on the planet. Lastly, it's your opportunity to sit in an exotic car that's worth twice your annual income.

## WINTER BLAST

A February family-oriented downtown event where attendees can ice-skate, take pictures with snowmen, drink hot chocolate, and try to forget the frigid weather. Bundle up!

## PACZKI DAY

It's Fat Tuesday everywhere in the world. In the Detroit area, it's when everyone loses their mind over *paczki* (pronounced "poonch-key," and that is the plural of *paczek*, pronounced "pohn-check"), which is fried dough with filling. Do not call it a doughnut. Paczki Day is a reflection of Polish heritage in the Detroit area, particularly in Hamtramck, which has bakeries that specialize in the delicacy.

## SPRING EVENTS

### ST. PATRICK'S DAY PARADE

In Corktown, Detroit's oldest neighborhood and a historically Irish enclave, everything turns green around St. Patrick's Day. The parade is actually unremarkable by parade standards, and Corktown residents are annoyed by the suburban invasion on the day, but with the right gang of people, you can still have a good time at the bars afterward.

### CINCO DE MAYO

OK, white people: it's not an excuse to get drunk on tequila with Mexicans. It is, however, an opportunity to absorb the culture of Mexicantown and southwest Detroit during the many events, including a parade, that go down on the day of the holiday and the days leading to it.

*The Nain Rouge*

### MARCHE DU NAIN ROUGE

The *nain rouge*, or red dwarf, is a mythical creature that is supposedly to blame for all of Detroit's woes. So each year in March, Detroiters stage a parade—and dress in funky costumes while doing so—to drive away the spirit of the *nain rouge*, who is blamed for everything from gentrification to that funny smell coming from Downriver.

### MOVEMENT

The annual homage to Detroit's electronic music legacy, you have to go to Movement even if you're not a fan of the genre. This ain't EDM on the radio, it's the real deal. And it'll get you moving. Ticket prices for the three-day experience are a bit steep (and the event used to be free back in the day), but no other festival draws an international crowd like Movement, rivaling even the likes of Coachella and Bonnaroo.

### DETROIT BELLE ISLE GRAND PRIX

The one time of year when a gorgeous park becomes a racetrack and annoys the greenthumbs. It has undergone some makeovers since its inception in 1982 and is now a champ car event. It's already on the to-do list for gearheads, but those curious about racing but not up for a trip to Indianapolis should stop by this event, usually held in May or June.

## SUMMER EVENTS

### MOTOR CITY PRIDE

Formerly housed in Ferndale, metro Detroit's gayest suburb, this June event got too big for the 'burbs and moved back to its rightful (if we're being honest) place downtown at Hart Plaza, lining up with other big-city pride events in June. The event regularly books indie pop stars and dance acts, as well as local musicians and performers popular among LBGT audiences.

### DOWNTOWN HOEDOWN

This annual country music festival has been a launching pad for several regional and national acts over the years, and has grown into a required stop for musicians building their career. One might not think Detroit would be a hub of country music, but just consider the number of residents with Southern roots, the popularity of country on the other side of the border, and the fact that we're in the midwest.

## DETROIT JAZZ FESTIVAL

A Labor Day weekend tradition, the jazz fest at Hart Plaza annually books some of the biggest names in the genre.

## INTERNATIONAL FREEDOM FESTIVAL

Better known to locals as "the fireworks" each year in June, and lining up with Canada Day and Independence Day. The fireworks are shot over the Detroit River so both Detroiters and Windsorites can enjoy. Some choose to go to the riverwalk or another nearby viewing area, but you can also watch from home on local TV.

## AFRICAN WORLD FESTIVAL

Every August, the African World Festival acts as a window into African and African-American culture. It is a celebration of African heritage especially, with dancers, singers, and other performers from the motherland.

## RIVER DAYS

For a weekend in June, attendees are invited to low-cost activities on Detroit's riverwalk, featuring concerts, water activities and plenty of kid-friendly fun. It's one of the more "small-town" events of the city.

## DALLY IN THE ALLEY

An annual September festival in Midtown—or Cass Corridor, depending on who you talk to. Dally is a street fair meant to encourage community among Detroiters, by exhibiting local artists, musicians, vendors, and other creatives. Some have argued that it's starting to feel just a *little* more corporate each year as Midtown grows in popularity, but it's still a fun time.

# FALL EVENTS

## DETROIT FREE PRESS MARATHON

Every big city has a marathon, and Detroit isn't any different—but part of this marathon's course goes across to Windsor, making it one of the few international marathons in the world. Each October, all of your Facebook friends get to show off that 26-mile accomplishment you've been meaning to train for, but just didn't get around to because you were drinking too many Soft Parades.

## AMERICA'S THANKSGIVING PARADE

It's one of the country's oldest Thanksgiving parades, right up there with the Macy's parade in New York City. For many Detroit kids, it's the first time they'll see Santa Claus before Christmas Eve—or the portraits at the mall, depending on your parenting style. Being a November event, you never know how cold it'll be if you actually want to attend, but it's also on local TV each year if you don't want to leave the house.

# YEAR-ROUND EVENTS

## DETROIT CITY FOOTBALL CLUB GAMES

So overnight, the DCFC soccer team became the heroes of young Detroit. When soccer season is here, DCFC fans put on their maroon and gold paraphernalia and cheer like hell for the guys on the field. Because the games are so energetic, even the most casual soccer fan is guaranteed to have a good time. Check out one game, at least.

# THE PEOPLE YOU ABSOLUTELY MUST BE FAMILIAR WITH

## MIKE DUGGAN

The current mayor of Detroit, Duggan was previously CEO of the Detroit Medical Center and also served as Wayne County Prosecutor and deputy Wayne County executive. He is "the white mayor," winning after a successful (and, frankly, unprecedented) write-in campaign he launched after failing to properly file paperwork to run for mayor. (Duggan had moved from the suburb of Livonia to Detroit a year before declaring himself a candidate, but filed the paperwork two weeks shy of the city's year-long residency requirement for mayoral candidates.) Duggan's goals for the city have been to eradicate blight, keep finances steady, and retain longtime residents by improving city services. The local media loves him because he drives his own car, a stark contrast to ex-mayor Kwame Kilpatrick's habit of buying cars on the city tab.

## DAN GILBERT

Founder of Quicken Loans and Rock Ventures, both among Detroit's largest employers, and owner of the Cleveland Cavaliers, which, very obviously, is not. An owner of several buildings downtown—colloquially called "Gilbertville" by a few snarky residents—Gilbert's goal is to draw as many people to downtown, be they residents or employees, as possible. Gilbert funds a private security force that monitors his downtown properties, something that quietly worries a few Detroiters due to general tensions with law enforcement, but has not been problematic thus far. Gilbert also writes emails in Comic Sans.

## MANUEL "MATTY" MOROUN

The billionaire owner of the Ambassador Bridge, which is notable because it is the only privately owned border crossing between the U.S. and Canada. Moroun's ownership of the bridge is a point of contention for locals, as he has thwarted public efforts over the years to construct a second bridge that would make life easier for both Americans and

Canadians (particularly when it comes to the automotive industry, as there are factories on both sides of the border). Moroun also owns the former Michigan Central Station in Corktown, and has let it deteriorate with no plans (as of now) to redevelop it—except for randomly putting in windows every now and then.

## MIKE ILITCH

Another billionaire, although Ilitch made his fortune from the Little Caesars chain of pizza restaurants, which he founded in the suburb of Garden City in 1959 (the same year Motown was founded!). Ilitch also owns the Detroit Tigers and Detroit Red Wings, and Olympia Entertainment, which owns the Fox Theatre and manages other venues in the area. Though Ilitch and his family are revered for revitalizing the Fox and keeping two sports teams in the city, a deal for a new hockey stadium (and several new residential and commercial buildings surrounding it) became controversial, as the deal could only be done if Detroit taxpayers footed the bill.

## JAMES CRAIG

A Detroit native, James Craig is the current chief of the Detroit Police Department, the latest in what seems to be revolving door of chiefs. There seems to never be a right time to assess the state of crime in Detroit, but Craig (so far) doesn't seem to be hampered by the same kind of personal or administrative mishaps that have dogged previous chiefs. The one thing to know about Craig, though, is that he isn't camera-shy; TV crews are always present for big crime raids that he leads.

## KYM WORTHY

As Wayne County Prosecutor, Worthy is front and center in the big, headline-grabbing cases in the area, from rapes to murders. Worthy shot to notoriety after successfully trying and convicting two white Detroit police officers, Walter Budzyn and Larry Nevers, in the beating death of a black Detroit man, Malice Green, during a traffic stop in 1992—just after the Rodney King beating in Los Angeles. Worthy further increased her profile after charging—a risky move in itself—former mayor Kwame Kilpatrick with eight felonies, which ultimately led to his downfall. Worthy's current mission is to deal with the Detroit Police Department's backlog of thousands of unprocessed rape kits, and bring justice to as many rape victims as possible.

## WARREN EVANS

Evans is the current Wayne County Executive, replacing the embattled Robert Ficano, most recently known for botching the construction of a county jail in downtown Detroit. Evans, who once was Wayne County Sheriff, also had a brief tenure as Detroit Police chief. During his run he—and a crew from a reality television show—was present during a home raid where a DPD officer shot and killed Aiyana Stanley-Jones, a seven-year-old girl who was sleeping on her couch during the melee. That still leaves a sour taste in some Detroiters' mouths.

## L. BROOKS PATTERSON

A thorn in the side of many Detroiters, Patterson has served as Oakland County Executive since the dawn of time (OK, 1992) and has lobbed anti-urban, latently racist rhetoric ever since. Oakland County became very commercial (and very wealthy) as residents and businesses left Detroit for the suburbs, yet now that more companies are reconsidering Detroit, Patterson feels threatened. Just ignore his constant jabs toward the city, but still enjoy what some of Oakland County's suburbs has to offer. (His less evil Macomb County counterpart is Mark Hackel.)

**“WHAT’S HAPPENING, WHAT UP, WHAT IT DO,”**
*that’s fa sho. But everybody in my city say,*
# WHAT UP DOE.

—Two Tone, “What Up Doe”

# CHAPTER 3

## DIFFICULT QUESTIONS ABOUT DETROIT WITH SIMPLE ANSWERS

A lot of people think coming to Detroit for the first time is just like when the Griswold family gets lost in East St. Louis in *National Lampoon's Vacation.* But I promise you won't be charged $5 for directions, and no one will paint "honky lips" on the side of your car.

### IS THE CITY EMPTY AND DESOLATE?

No.

### ARE CERTAIN PARTS OF THE CITY EMPTY AND DESOLATE?

Yes.

### IS DETROIT LAWLESS?

No. Buckle up. Drive the speed limit. Don't fight anyone in the streets. (Jaywalking is not a crime, but use the crosswalks, anyway. People drive batshit crazy, sometimes.)

## DOES EVERYONE IN DETROIT OWN A GUN?

No.

## SHOULD I BUY A GUN?

You have the right to, sure.

## IS IT TRUE I SHOULDN'T GO TO CERTAIN NEIGHBORHOODS?

Generally the police think that if you are white and going into places known for drug trafficking, you might be a suburbanite buying drugs. But unless you see a "no [racial group] allowed," no. (Spoiler: You won't.)

## WHAT ARE THE CHANCES OF ME BEING SHOT IN DETROIT?

Pretty high if:

- You are shooting at someone else with a gun.
- You are shooting yourself with a gun.
- You are attempting to burglarize the home of a gun owner.
- You are engaged in the drug trade and make yourself a target.
- You bring any other trouble upon yourself by committing high-stakes crimes.

If none of these apply, you should be fine.

## WHERE ARE THE GOOD NEIGHBORHOODS?

Oh, do you mean Corktown, Midtown, and Woodbridge? Because when people say "good" neighborhoods in Detroit, "good" is code for "where the white people live." Go on any message board or online forum, and Corktown, Midtown, and Woodbridge are the stock answers to people asking where they should live in Detroit. Know that these answers are always given because, well, this is where the white people live. The new white people. There are white people all over Detroit, but the ones that are new are moving here. And thus, people conflate "young and white" with "I can leave my doors unlocked." You cannot. You don't leave your doors unlocked in Detroit, first of all. This isn't the small town you grew up in and it never will be. But you cannot conflate "white" with "safe," because there are several—*several!*—"safe" neighborhoods that just happen to be full of blacks, Latinos, and other minorities.

## WHAT ARE THE "TWO DETROITS" I'VE HEARD OF?

"Two Detroits" is a newer term to describe what's going on here at the moment. "Old Detroit" represents the longtime residents. Then there's the other part of Detroit, "New Detroit," that represents newer residents.

## WHAT'S "OLD DETROIT"?

It can be a pejorative term for people who have lived in the city for a significant amount of time. Some people group everyone—especially residents of color—into this category if they don't live in Downtown or Midtown, not knowing that there are plenty of neighborhoods outside the central business district doing just fine. Some people use it to describe an obstructionist who argues against progress. And some people just use it as a descriptor for poor people.

## WHAT'S "NEW DETROIT"?

When people say "New Detroit," they usually use it as a pejorative as well. It can mean a hipster who just moved here. It can mean any young person that just moved here. It can mean any white person that just moved here, hipster or not, young or old. It is often used to describe someone who appears to be in Detroit to further their own self-interest and not the interests of the community at large. In other words, someone who is obviously in favor of gentrification, whether they spell it out or not, or someone who wants to challenge a longstanding tradition without consulting their neighbors first. Or, simply, just a jackass.

## IS GENTRIFICATION HAPPENING IN DETROIT?

At a gradual pace, yes. There have been pronounced examples of building owners turning low-income and/or senior residences into market-rate housing for anyone who can afford to pay the newly increased rates. But Detroit isn't that unrecognizable yet. We have not experienced the rapid flipping of blocks, as in some New York City or Austin, Texas, neighborhoods, because the city is still very, very vacant. Detroit is, however, in a position to solve a gentrification problem before it happens. Some residents also refer to a certain "psychological gentrification," in which the hopes and wishes of existing residents are pushed aside in favor of attracting younger, trendier residents of any background.

## HOW DO YOU TALK LIKE A DETROITER?

Say "pop," not "soda" or "Coke." Pronounce it "duh-troyt," not "dee-troyt." "Down south" is anything south of the Mason-Dixon line, but "up north" is anything north of Flint. And please know that we don't use the same slang as rappers in other regions. For example, a "bando" is what people in Atlanta and other points South say for an abandoned house. We call an abandoned house an abandoned house. We might say "trap" to represent where someone might buy drugs or we might call it a "spot." And we call lots of things "spots" here – the Chinese spot, the Mexican spot, the Puerto Rican spot. A spot can be a club, a restaurant, anywhere that's chill.

## WHO IS COLEMAN YOUNG?

The first black mayor of Detroit. He took office in 1974 and left office in 1994. He died in 1998.

## WAS COLEMAN YOUNG THE REASON WHY WHITE PEOPLE LEFT DETROIT?

Yes and no. White people were already leaving Detroit when he took office. And some white people left just because he took office.

*Coleman Young*
*Mayor of Detroit, 1974-1994*

## DID COLEMAN YOUNG TELL WHITE PEOPLE TO LEAVE DETROIT?

Absolutely not. You may have heard a famous statement from Young, said during his inauguration: "I issue a forward warning now to all those pushers, to all rip-off artists, to all muggers: It's time to leave Detroit; hit Eight Mile Road! And I don't give a damn if they are black or white, or if they wear Superfly suits or blue uniforms with silver badges. Hit the road." This was not, as many people have tried to interpret it over the years, a proclamation for white people to cross Eight Mile Road and never come back. It was, as Young stated, a warning to criminals that they were no longer welcome in the city.

## IF COLEMAN YOUNG WAS SUCH A GOOD MAYOR, WHY IS DETROIT THE WAY IT IS NOW?

For several reasons. The *Detroit Free Press* has done an excellent analysis called "How Detroit Went Broke," and it had little do with Young, actually. The whole thing is a must-read for newcomers, but in short: mayors before Young did not cut any city expenses as the population decreased. When expenses kept ballooning over the years, mayors after Young still did not cut any city expenses or stop borrowing money to cover increasing debts. What bit Detroit in the ass was covering pensions for retirees, having to pay back millions in loans, and cutting services to the bone at the last minute instead of gradually cutting over the years to reflect the now-decreased population.

## BUT ARE THERE WILD DOGS TAKING OVER DETROIT?

No.

## IS DETROIT BEING TAKEN OVER BY OTHER FORMS OF WILDLIFE?

No, although nature does run its course on abandoned plots of land. Weeds grow tall, brush gets thick, and the most wild of beings—pheasants, noisy, noisy pheasants—make their nests. That's about it. Rabbits, possums, skunks, and raccoons can be seen on occasion. It is extremely rare to see as much as a deer. Anything other than that is generally unheard of.

## DOES THE CITY PLOW STREETS IN THE WINTER?

Sometimes they do, sometimes they don't. And sometimes the responsibility falls on the county. Be prepared, and consider snow tires.

## DOES THE WEATHER IN MICHIGAN REALLY CHANGE DAY TO DAY WITHOUT WARNING?

Yes. One day it'll be 80 and sunny. The next it'll be 50 and raining.

## IS MOTOWN STILL IN DETROIT?

Motown moved its headquarters from Detroit to Los Angeles in the 1970s. There's a significant faction of the population that hates Berry Gordy for it, but still loves the music regardless. Many of the artists moved out of Detroit as well.

## WILL MY TRASH BE PICKED UP ON TIME?

Most of the time.

## WILL MY CAR BE STOLEN?

Your car is always at risk of being stolen no matter where you take it.

## WHAT ARE ALL THOSE STUFFED ANIMALS DOING TIED TO THAT UTILITY POLE/TREE/LIGHT POST?

Those are memorials—sometimes, unfortunately, called "murder bears"—to signify where someone was killed, by accident or by intent.

## ARE THERE CERTAIN PRECAUTIONS I CAN TAKE TO PREVENT MY CAR FROM BEING STOLEN OR VANDALIZED?

Live in a place with a garage. If not, use a steering-wheel lock and wheel locks. Don't leave valuables in your car regardless.

## DOES EMINEM LIVE IN DETROIT?

He's known to live in the suburbs but he's also very secretive so maybe, maybe not?

## IS EIGHT MILE DANGEROUS?

Sure, if you put yourself in danger on Eight Mile, like attempting to rob a bank on Eight Mile or sell drugs to strangers on Eight Mile.

## DOES EVERYONE WORK FOR THE CAR COMPANIES?

No. Many people do, but not everyone.

## DO THEY ACTUALLY BUILD CARS IN DETROIT?

Yes. Not all of them, but a few models are built in factories here.

## WILL I BE TERRORIZED FOR DRIVING A FOREIGN CAR?

No. See Chapter 8 for more.

## IS EVERYONE IN DETROIT ILLITERATE?

Some people are, like any other city. However, there's a nasty statistic going around that 47% of Detroiters are illiterate. This stat started circulating in 2011 as new information, but the data was actually from a study done in 1998. Regardless, this is a factoid you should not repeat while we wait for a concrete study detailing just how big (or how small?) that number truly is.

## CAN YOU BUY A HOUSE FOR ONE DOLLAR?

Yes, but you wouldn't want to. See Chapter 14 for more.

## DO THE POLICE TAKE A LONG TIME TO RESPOND TO A CALL?

Lately, not really. In the past, they would. Now, it depends on how urgent the situation. Life-threatening situations receive timely responses. Non-threatening responses may vary.

## DID BLACK POLITICIANS RUIN DETROIT?

Oh, God. No.

## SO WAIT, WHAT HAPPENED TO DETROIT, AGAIN?

Long story short: white flight, ineffective policies put in place long before any of us were born, and too-heavy of a dependence placed on the automotive industry.

## WHAT HAPPENED WITH KWAME KILPATRICK?

Our former mayor couldn't keep his hand out of the cookie jar. He couldn't keep his dick in his pants, either, but neither his hand nor his dick made Detroit the way it is today. The storm had been brewing long before he took office. A few things on the extremely long list of reasons why Kilpatrick is serving federal prison time and owes a restitution to the city of Detroit: Using city funds to pay for dinners and hotel rooms tied to his extramarital affair, lying about using said city funds under oath, having a secret slush fund, tax evasion, bribery, fraud, getting kickbacks for his friends, and being completely selfish and arrogant about it the entire time.

### DO PEOPLE HATE THE FACT THAT THERE IS A WHITE MAYOR NOW?

No. In this particular case, we can always agree that the best man for the job is the best man for the job. That sounds like the Republican's default answer to why we still have affirmative action, I know. But when Mayor Mike Duggan was still in stumping mode, his opponents weren't the strongest.

### WHY DO PEOPLE IN THE SUBURBS HATE DETROIT?

Ask them.

### WHAT'S THAT SMELL?

I don't know. The incinerator? A coffee plant? The sins of our ancestors? It's Detroit, it smells like a lot of things at any given moment.

### WHEN WILL DETROIT FINALLY REBOUND?

After you die.

## YOUR FIRST DETROIT PARTY

When you go to a party in Detroit, practice this phrase: "*speramus meliora, resurget cineribus.*" It's Latin for "We hope for better things, it will rise from the ashes." It's the city of Detroit's motto, and it's also the catchphrase of every newcomer who has lived here for five minutes.

We've got a lot of interesting characters here, so here's how to interact with some of the esteemed guests.

## BLACK REPUBLICAN

Certainly there's nothing wrong with conservative views, but Detroit is a very liberal city and they may not quite fit in. But there's a new breed of "pull-yourself-up-by-your-bootstraps" blacks emerging in Detroit. He may have grown up in the 'hood, or maybe the suburbs. You can't always tell. You can tell by his actions: he thinks that our socioeconomic travesty is linked to personal choice and not decades of conditioning, and is empowered by being embraced by white co-workers or friends.

## MADONNA

Not the pop star herself, but the type of person who leaves the Detroit suburbs and swears that living in the Detroit suburbs was the worst thing on earth. She loves urban life in the city, but spends every moment bashing her white-picket upbringing. Life in the suburbs was just *sooooo* bland and they just don't understand why people don't give Detroit a chance. There are reasons why if you read on. (For more on Madonnas, see Chapter 7.)

## THE SOCIALITE

She's that girl born and raised in the city who never left. She lives on the west side and has cousins, ex-boyfriends, and besties all on that side of town (Dexter, Seven Mile, Schoolcraft, Joy Road, Puritan, Evergreen). Or she lives on the east side and has cousins, ex-boyfriends, and besties on that side of town (Dequindre, Seven Mile, Mack, Cadieux, Chandler Park, Gratiot). Thousands of followers on Instagram. A favorite in the boutiques. Body and hair always on point – hell, maybe she *does* hair. Might have a degree, might not, but street smart all the way. Sweet as pie until you do her wrong. Could probably throw down on the grill if you asked her to. Knows the city in and out.

## THE GENUINE ARTIST

No discernible source of income since he's basically living off grants, the genuine artist has a deep appreciation of Detroit culture and knows how to express it without distilling the voices of those who have been here. He could be a College of Creative Studies grad or dropout. Maybe has some part-time work here or there. Always has good weed, though.

## THE CHEAP-RENT ARTIST

Complete opposite of the genuine artist, he's just here because they heard Detroit is cheap. Lives in a bubble with other artists, is way too optimistic about his purpose here, and always, always gets things wrong about Detroit. Sure, he can paint, but can he understand that a painting can't get a block's streetlights turned back on?

## THE WIDE-EYED STUDENT

Is likely spending a summer here with some volunteer program, or maybe is an intern at Quicken Loans. Already knows all the hip places to go because she's been following popular Detroit Instagrammers for weeks before arriving here. Everything is just so new and exciting! Then she lives here for a while and becomes jaded like the rest of us.

## HIPPIE GRANNY

She protested everything there was to protest in the 1960s, took a break to raise a family in the 70s, and then went right back to being a badass when the kids were grown. She loves granola and New Age healing, and reluctantly accepts the new Whole Foods although deep down she knows there may be some ripple effects there. Maybe she runs a book club, maybe she runs a yoga group, or maybe she puts out a newsletter detailing all the injustices going on around the world.

## THE CONSPIRACY THEORIST

Everything is an evil, sinister plot to take over Detroit. He will tell you about the systematic disinvestment in the neighborhoods that began with redlining. He will tell you about how the schools were destroyed by a combination of unfair ordinances and gubernatorial abandonment. He will talk about how politicians on both the local and state level are in on a scheme to sell Detroit to the highest bidder. He will sound crazy, but you should listen to every word, because there are grains of truth hiding in there.

## OVERENTHUSIASTIC SUBURBAN TRANSPLANT

"Oh, my God! I *just* got a job downtown and they *just* opened this new restaurant and I *just* signed a lease on a great new place and they're *just* about to put in the new rail system and I *just* had a great ride on the People Mover and I *just* joined this great new gym and everything is just so fantastic in the city of Detroit! Even though my grandparents booked it for the suburbs right after the riot and I haven't been alive long enough to really witness Detroit's downward spiral, I really feel like the city is coming back this time!"

## MIDDLE-AGED WHITE GUY WHO LIVED OUTSIDE THE CITY FOR YEARS AND SUDDENLY MOVED HERE

He's the guy that has a varied, but insightful outlook on the city. He likely was born here, or maybe he was born far away from Michigan, but spent a good chunk of his youth here. He lived in one of the suburbs for a long time, and *something*—a divorce, an empty nest, a desire to no longer hide his suppressed homosexuality—prompted him to take the leap into the city. Generally people from the suburbs have a terribly skewed view of Detroit, but this guy has a balanced, measured view of why things are the way they are.

## URBAN SCHOLAR

The person who has lived in Detroit for two years but knows the history of the city dating back 200 years. Everything about Detroit can be explained away with data and numbers and statistics, and the future of Detroit can only be determined by the same thing. While numbers can be helpful—and it's nice to have statistics to back up an argument (or support your own biases)—Detroit's new wave of amateur urban planners sometimes forget that there are actual people behind the numbers. Humans have varied stories, but getting too wrapped up in statistics in a city so divided on several lines can often perpetuate stereotypes.

## TEACHER

Likely came to Detroit via Teach for America or some other similar program, and has had a firsthand look at Detroit's youth because of it. He's going to fall into one of two categories: The *Dangerous Minds* savior who believes he's going to save these kids' lives (avoid) or the pragmatist who really cares about her students, but is realistic about the challenges they face. Either way, it seems like there are a lot of teachers in Detroit lately, but not that many schools. (For more on schools, turn to Chapter 12.)

## THE CURMUDGEON

Pessimistic, sarcastic and cynical about everything new going on in Detroit—possibly with good reason. She may be skeptical about Detroit's revival because some of its effects can lead to gentrification and the abandonment of many long-term residents. Or she many not like some of the renaissance because it's cool to be anti-establishment.

## HOMETOWN BOY DONE GOOD

Under 30 and already has his shit together. Likely a third- or fourth-generation Detroiter, works for the city or state, and either just got married or has been married and now expecting. Is probably in a midlevel job for now, but will be a state representative or a city councilperson in a few election cycles. We're seeing lately several new political types who have witnessed the corruption of the past and want to help the city start anew. For lack of a better term, they're "the ones to watch."

## THE MULTITASKER

She owns like five businesses, three houses, just bought a building, saved a family from a burning apartment, and is going to be on the front page of *Metro Times* next week. Goddamn, how does she find time for it all? If you meet this person at a party, she has a) likely taken advantage of rock-bottom prices to amass a nice portfolio of Detroit properties and b) only had time for this one party, so you better get in her brain now while you can. (To learn how not to be insanely jealous of these overachievers, turn to Chapter 16.)

## THE CAUTIOUS FERNDALE RESIDENT

"You know, we're really thinking about moving into the city, but not right now." He's been on the fence about moving from the suburbs into Detroit for a few years now, but something is always holding him back. First he was worried about crime. Then he was worried about property values. Then he was worried about the bankruptcy. Then he had a neighborhood in mind, but a great rental just opened up in his suburb. He really, really wants to give Detroit a go, but most likely won't. He does love hanging out in Detroit as much as he can, however, and should be respected for doing so. (For more on city-suburb relations, turn to Chapter 7.)

## SOMEONE ELSE'S EX

Listen, Detroit might be a city of thousands, but the dating pool gets really shallow, really fast. There's a lot of self-segregation: New Detroiters tend to date fellow New Detroiters, suburban transplants tend to date fellow suburbanites, and so on, and so forth. There won't be any Jerry Springer-type drama, but there might be a bit of juicy gossip.

## THE DOCUMENTARIAN

That person who carries a camera everywhere, especially to Eastern Market. She's either working on a photographic essay, or a full-fledged film. Documentaries are what's hot right now in Detroit—there's a new one online every week! Always be dressed to impressed, because you never know when you'll be in the lens.

## THE REVOLUTIONARY

Always in close contact with the conspiracy theorist, the revolutionary is ready for social upheaval at any minute—just as soon as he finishes that pour-over. You can find this person tweeting nonstop about injustices in Detroit and wondering out loud if anything's going to be done to stop it. Problem is, sometimes these efforts feel like bandwagon jumping, and chances are our revolutionary won't be so revolutionary once he lands a plum job at a nonprofit or some other community organization.

## THE DEVELOPER

"Yeah, I just bought another duplex." This person owns a bunch of properties all around the city, which is easy to do now since everything is so cheap. Listen to him, though—he has insights on what life is like in whatever neighborhoods he's investing in.

## THE FARMER

All dirty fingernails and faded jeans, the farmer is a growing presence in Detroit, taking empty plots of land and making them sustainable. Some are old-school, tilling the soil like generations before them, and some may be using fancy-schmancy technology to get the job done. Either way it goes, she has an iPhone. Old McDonald, now with Instagram.

*I hear outsiders talking about a "new Detroit"*

**WHEN I REMEMBER THE BEAUTY OF**

# OLD DETROIT.

—jessica Care moore, poet

# CHAPTER 4

## HOW NOT TO OFFEND PEOPLE WHEN TALKING ABOUT DETROIT

Detroiters are sensitive, for good reason. Detroiters are humans with feelings, and humans worthy of allowance to feel. For that reason, it is easy to take something the wrong way and feel slighted. Detroiters are easily offended, and that's because they are fighting to control how they express their feelings when they've constantly been told how to feel by so many others, be it the county executive who spits on them for merely existing to the presidential hopeful who suggests the city should just be wiped away.

There are several competing narratives in Detroit. There is the "all Detroit's residents are dirty and poor and in desperate need of a white savior" narrative. There is the "Detroit was a blank canvas (before the white people came)" narrative. There is the "black people don't want change in Detroit" narrative. And there are even more nuanced tales being spun daily. Each one is competing for attention as more residents pour into empty domiciles with extravagant ideas and intense social media debates force us to ruthlessly choose sides based on whose online barbs are the strongest. Strip away the flowery buzzwords and tired tropes, and several of the prevailing opinions out there are rooted in flawed relationships between Detroit and the rest of the country, Detroit and Michigan, Detroit and its suburbs, Detroit and its residents, Detroit and its culture, maybe even Detroit and itself.

There are ways to avoid offending, though: Use common sense.

Be wily; be smart. Know where you're coming from with your thoughts, and understand that the place where you're coming from is perhaps much different than the place you're in now. Entering into a conversation with a Detroiter can quickly escalate into a sticky, awkward experience, but there are landmines you can avoid. Be compassionate; be honest. And understand that humor—sometimes even self-depreciation—can go a long way, maybe even ease the awkwardness a little.

## "I KNOW EVERYONE IN TOWN."

There are, at any given moment, well more than half a million people living in Detroit. No, you don't know everyone here. Once, a local business owner complained to a food writer about the service at a new bar that got buckets of media coverage in the run-up to its grand opening. Per this business owner's gripes, the bar's service was slow and orders were forgotten. The entrepreneur told the bar's management that she "knows everyone in town" and cautioned that her word would get around fast. Sometimes saying things like that can come off spiteful, if we're being honest. The Detroiter who claims to know "everyone" is either referring to all the white people they know (which, again, can't be that many in a mostly black city) or trying to throw around weight they don't have. Don't be that person.

## "DO YOU KNOW WHO I AM?"

What, are we supposed to know who your father is, too? A more vulgar version of the homie-dontcha-know-me was uttered by Christine Beatty, the former chief of staff (and longtime mistress) of ex-mayor Kwame Kilpatrick. In 2004, when stopped by a city police officer in the midst of Kilpatrick's first term, Ms. Beatty exclaimed, "Do you know who the fuck I am?" That's now a punchy Detroit catchphrase, but believe it or not there are Detroit "celebrities" high and low on the totem pole who try to push through this small pond on their name alone. If you become the next startup zillionaire here, don't play this card.

## "I KNOW WHAT IT'S LIKE TO GROW UP IN DETROIT BECAUSE…"

A phrase uttered far too often by either new Detroiters who have grown up in the suburbs but had parents that worked in the city in some capacity, or folks who grew up poor outside Detroit. It's certainly OK to describe what it's like to live in Detroit if you have lived here for some time. But there are also certainly Detroiters who would take offense at endless comparisons of your suburban or non-Detroit upbringing with theirs. This also applies to transplants from other cities; the experiences here in Detroit are like none other.

## "OUR SHARED STRUGGLES/CHALLENGES/HEARTBREAKS"

Geez, do you think all Detroiters wallow in misery 24/7? Let's also talk about our shared joys and celebrations, you Debbie Downer, you. (Also, maybe the best way to get on someone's good side is not to immediately focus on the negative?)

## "THIS CITY IS A BLANK CANVAS/BLANK SLATE" OR "THERE WAS NOTHING HERE BEFORE…"

A few years ago in the business publication *Crain's Detroit Business*, two of the city's up-and-coming entrepreneurs simultaneously commented that Detroit offered endless opportunity for like-minded business owners because the city was a "blank canvas." Initially meant as a metaphor for filling in empty spaces, the "blank canvas" idea has taken off like a rocket, becoming a catchphrase for the wannabe hopeful looking for a quick pull quote. Longtime residents bristle at this term, seeing as the city was never "blank" to begin with. There were people in the neighborhoods where these entrepreneurs started opening up shop, and the "canvas" was filled with the history that came before they arrived. To say the city is "blank" is a total erasure of the city's colorful past.

## "THERE IS NO SUCH THING AS GENTRIFICATION IN DETROIT" OR "THERE AREN'T ENOUGH PEOPLE IN DETROIT FOR GENTRIFICATION TO HAPPEN."

When people hear this, what they're really hearing is: "There aren't enough white people in Detroit for gentrification to happen." There is a lot of vacancy in Detroit, which is why the latter sentiment has taken off. But gentrification is happening, and there is no one type of person who causes it.

## "WHAT DETROIT REALLY NEEDS RIGHT NOW IS..."

Good schools, good people filling empty houses. That's how you finish that sentence. Now, there are plenty of things that *would be nice to have* in Detroit. But be conscious that when using the "this city needs" construction, you're not just thinking of what you and your friends need to survive in this town.

## "CAN ____ SAVE DETROIT?"

No. It can't. For the last few years, entrepreneurs have sought a silver bullet to fix Detroit's problems, leading many to think they're on a crusade to rescue this city from ... whatever will make them feel better about themselves. A few years back, five cheery Texans released a video describing their plans to open a coffee shop in a "slum community" to "start an artistic revival"; teach in schools to "love on kids that have never experienced love ... to let them know they are worthy"; and "rebuilding ancient ruins and devastations"... all because "God put it in their hearts." Needless to say, the video was panned, not just because of the saccharine of it all, but because when you ride in on a white horse to tell a city full of poor black people exactly what they need to be saved, you come off as self-righteous and ignorant.

## "YOU ACTUALLY DON'T NEED A CAR."

That's easy to say if you are single, physically fit, live within walking distance of everything you need, and are not averse to rapidly changing weather conditions. However, to be condescending to Detroiters who actually do need a car or truck just because you found it way to make it work without one is heavily shortsighted.

## "YOU DON'T WANT TO TAKE THE BUS ANYWHERE."

Why yes, Mr. My Bike Gets Me Everywhere, *you* don't want to take the bus anywhere, because you don't have to. Yet for the thousands of Detroiters who do rely on public transit—many for reasons similar to the car situation above—to reach places further than a bike would carry someone, "not taking the bus" isn't an easy out.

## "THE BLACK COMMUNITY..."

Wait, are you black? No? Then, don't assume to speak to the needs of the "community." And by the way, blacks in Detroit (like everywhere else in America) are not monolithic. Same with Latinos. Same with Arabs. (See also: "I have friends that are black.")

## "WHAT ARE YOU DOING FOR DETROIT?"

Here's a question often asked by superboosters who bristle at the slightest criticism of politics, business, or goodwill in the city. It reeks of the kind of self-satisfaction that comes from doing something that would be relatively mediocre in any other city in the world. Oh, so you planted a tree during a nature event in an urban forest: good for you! It doesn't mean that the person who still lives and works in the city is doing any less. Everyone contributes to this city in their own way—and keep in mind there's no age or time limit for doing something that you'd consider a great accomplishment.

## "IT'S OK TO RUN THE STOP LIGHTS BECAUSE THE COPS WON'T PULL YOU OVER."

Once, on St. Patrick's Day (and not under the influence, FYI), I was pulled over for speeding *juuuuust* over the limit to beat a yellow light. In some areas of Detroit, you can get stopped for this. However, the notion that all traffic signals can be disobeyed is wrongfully passed among a certain subset of the population. The city is not lawless, and treating it as such does not make for a functional city. Moreover, the disproportionate treatment of Americans of color by police in any kind of situation should be cause for those more privileged to not encourage anyone to break the law, even if it is a measly traffic signal.

## "WHY DON'T THE POLICE FOCUS ON MORE IMPORTANT CRIMES?"

In this town, this translates to, "Why don't the police focus more on arresting minorities?" The "more important crimes" debate crops up when the authorities—police or otherwise—begin cracking down on nonviolent crimes such as graffiti and traffic violations. But the law is the law, and you have to realize that in order to make this a functioning city again, it means not treating it as a lawless free-for-all.

## "WE WON'T BE A WORLD-CLASS CITY UNTIL..."

Until what, exactly? Detroit is the city that put the world on wheels. That notoriety is strong enough in itself. But comparing Detroit to other cities (particularly larger ones like Tokyo or New York City) is unfair to Detroit. You can be a much better Detroiter by letting Detroit be Detroit.

## "SHOULDN'T IT BE ALL BUSINESSES/RESIDENTS?"

A regular concern of longtime residents is that minority-owned businesses, particularly black-owned businesses, be included, and even prioritized, in the revival of Detroit. Critics of this ideal, often white, say they are tired of being scolded for their participation in the economic revival and often answer with the retort, "We're all Detroiters no matter what!" But it's problematic when black businesses and residents across the country, not just in Detroit, have had a harder hill to climb when it comes to equality. So yes, special attention must be paid to minorities until the playing field is level. (Think of the #alllivesmatter hashtag that began circulating in response to the #blacklivesmatter movement protesting police killings in 2014. Saying #alllivesmatter greatly diminishes the struggles of black Americans, doesn't it?)

## "THEY SHOULD JUST PAVE THAT PLACE OVER AND..."

There was talk among city officials in the late aughts and early 2010s of clearing out entire neighborhoods and moving the residents to other, more populated neighborhoods. Those notions have died down as the city rethinks its best practices to include repopulating the more devastated areas, but it's still an idea among pie-in-the-sky idealists who think urban removal is the key to Detroit's problems. There are people in those neighborhoods. They will decide what is their best option.

## "CAN'T THEY JUST BUY A BETTER CAR?"

A lot of people in Detroit drive really, really raggedy shitboxes—as do people in a lot of urban cities. But it takes them where they need to go. Their jobs, their doctors' appointments, their kids' schools. Would you rather they not drive at all?

*Political power itself is always in danger when you don't have economic power… The principal levers of power are basically in the hands of whites.*

---

**TO SAVE THIS CITY** *is to save the best chance we have at* **COMBINING POLITICAL** *AND* **ECONOMIC POWER.**

—Arthur Johnson, civil rights activist

# CHAPTER 5

## HOW YOU SHOULD BE TALKING ABOUT DETROIT

Every year on Mackinac Island, a resort spot in Lake Huron, off the Upper Peninsula of Michigan, the Detroit Regional Chamber—something akin to a downtown development agency—holds an annual gathering called the Mackinac Policy Conference. It is a gathering of business leaders, politicians from across the state, movers, shakers, the journalists who cover all of the above, and immigrant service workers who spend a few days on the island discussing exactly what the conference is named for: policy. They discuss social policy. Education policy. Financial policy. Tax policy. Infrastructure policy. Policy policy. It is said this is the site of backroom deals, but lately deals are made out in the open in front of the press. And as the conference has gotten more attention it has morphed into Michigan's own White House Correspondents' Dinner.

MPC hasn't reached TMZ-level coverage yet, but it's getting there. Each year, reporters have increasingly abandoned journalistic ethics to cozy up closer with sources; look no further than the barrage of selfies pumped out each year by reporters on the island, either with each other or the very subjects they must turn a critical eye toward after the party's over. And then there are the endless freebies. All the J-school rules are left on the Lower Peninsula when there's free, Detroit-made bourbon to sip and Mackinac Island fudge to take home to the kiddies.

The crux of the conference is conversation. Conversations about policy, of course, but also conversations about whatever pressing issue is facing the state of Michigan at the moment. Are state test scores low among fourth-graders? Conversation about it. Is there a brain drain as younger residents move to Chicago, as they usually do? Conversation about it.

The Mackinac Policy Conference, despite being hosted by a Detroit-based organization, draws a mostly white crowd, but of late the conversations have turned to race relations in Detroit and other Michigan cities. Being a business conference, the conversations about race have little to do with actual interactions between, say, Latinos and whites or Arabs and blacks, but rather how any one group's spending power impacts development in the state. And these conversations about race in Michigan, and especially in Detroit, are all based around what's convenient for white people. I mean, the MPC is held at a resort in a hotel, far away from Detroit's problems. How are the people there supposed to talk about Detroit's problems when they're so removed from it?

More often than not, it seems the proposed solution for white people's problems—be they problems that impact white people directly, or problems with other racial groups that have ripple effects on whites—is conversation.

Now, I'm a cynic and I'm a skeptic. Maybe I was born with these characteristics. Or maybe they just came to me by circumstance. Being born a minority in this country and realizing your stance later on makes you this way. But here's how these conversations typically go in Detroit: there'll be a panel discussion hosted by savvy urbanites, where the panel talks about their experiences. Concerns are aired, but often ignored. Actions rarely result from these conversations, it just makes people feel good that they tried to make an effort. Once these conversations are over, they are forgotten. And it's easy to remain cynical and skeptical.

Too much cynicism and skepticism can be dangerous, though. They are useful traits to have, but when they cloud your sense of optimism, you can easily find yourself living in misery and wondering how you got there.

I did have an unexpected but fruitful conversation with someone recently. We're friends, we both live in the city, and we both ultimately want the same thing from Detroit: for it to be a functional, fun place to live. The thing is, we didn't even set out to talk about Detroit. But you know how it is when friends talk, the conversation can go in several different directions.

It's not that I don't talk about Detroit in real life, it's just that my friends and I are often so cynical and skeptical. We've all seen it all before: broken promises from politicians, false starts in the economy, putting faith in this store here or that restaurant there. And sometimes talking about Detroit can be tiring.

But now that it's starting to feel like things are—finally!—changing for the better in Detroit, this conversation felt oddly optimistic, something I hadn't felt in so long, I actually walked away feeling refreshed. We talked about our personal lives and ambitions, and how they are both tied to the future of the city. Not once did we talk about moving elsewhere, as so often is the case when younger Michiganders start talking about where they'll be in the next few years. No, we both saw things on the horizon that would make us want to stay.

We were honest, which is necessary. And we were realistic. We both know functionality isn't coming tomorrow. But we both kept saying, "Man, in a couple of years…"

But perhaps the most interesting thing about this conversation was that the intimacy allowed not only our honesty, but a chance to listen to each other.

There's a scene in the Jackson family miniseries *The Jacksons: An American Dream* where a young Michael Jackson is invited to sing on stage with Motown grand diva Diana Ross. The two duet on "Reach Out and Touch (Somebody's Hand)," Ross' first solo outing after leaving the Supremes.

As the supposedly based-on-a-true-story TV movie would have you believe, Jackson stole the show from Ross, singing the second verse of the song and refusing to give her back her microphone, causing them to have a friendly tug-of-war on stage. Jackson continued to out-sing Ross on her own song, with his parents and siblings looking on from the audience.

It's a strange metaphor I'm going to present here, and you kind of have to watch it to get the whole gist. But when you have a newcomer like MJ upstaging a veteran like Diana, and not sharing the stage, it's reminding me of the narrative here in Detroit right now.

Without taking an official census or survey, I can guarantee that there is no one in Detroit who wants things to stay the way they are. Little old women do not wake up and say, "You know, I really hope they don't tear down that abandoned house that's now a dope house." No one ever says, "We don't need better schools and police."

And no one ever says that Detroit doesn't need more people. Depending on your figures, the city is anywhere between 60% to 80% occupied—both figures way too small for a 139-square-mile city, seeing that there is not a large enough population to support the services that are needed for this land mass.

No Detroiter turns their nose up to new business, either. Everyone here might not have sophisticated financial acumen (I certainly don't), but people do realize the basics of what investment brings. Some may look at new business as slowly restoring an eroding tax base, and some may have a more simplistic view of having a new place to patronize.

But I can guarantee that what every Detroiter wants is a chance to be heard, and this is where that Ross-Jackson metaphor comes into play. By sharing the stage, and sharing the microphone, we all have a chance to express ourselves. Share our fears, our doubts, our hopes, and our wishes.

Sharing and listening is what can make Detroit better—on both sides. But it's better if that's done in a close setting. Maybe that's why I've been cynical and skeptical, because so much of the conversation about Detroit has been led by people I don't know or recognize. But once you sit down and talk with someone and have that real dialogue, there's absolutely nothing like it.

**THE POPULAR WAY TO EXPLAIN THE DECLINE OF DETROIT—** *that is, the one so ardently talked up within certain white circles and media, if I may risk being redundant — is to*

# PIN IT ALL ON ME.

—Coleman Young, *Hard Stuff*

# CHAPTER 6

## HOW TO BE WHITE IN DETROIT

When you move to Detroit, you are immersing yourself in black history by default. For white people who have decided to live in Detroit, you will have to contend with some of the historic and present tensions here.

There was a lunch table at my high school that we called the "White Girl Table." It's self-explanatory: Our school was almost 100% black, except for the handful of white girls that sat together at lunch. Someone could have easily written *Why Are All The White Kids Sitting Together At The Cafeteria?* about our high school, a flip on the popular sociology book.

The white girls in our school were scattered across the city. Some lived in Warrendale, a southern Detroit neighborhood that borders Dearborn; some in Southwest Detroit; some in Rosedale Park, a northwest neighborhood filled with 1940s colonials; some in Jefferson-Chalmers, a weathered east-side district near the Detroit River.

There was nothing wrong with having a White Girl Table at our school, but I can imagine how it could be strange for some of my classmates who'd barely interacted with white people before high school. Back then, some elementary and middle schools didn't have a single white student. If you are black in Detroit and surrounded by black people 24/7, and the only thing you know about white people is that they once owned slaves a hundred years ago, holding hands and singing "We Are The World" with them in high school probably isn't at the top of your mind.

Although most people moving to Detroit think that all the white people left town after the 1967 riots, hundreds of white families stayed in the city, particularly in south and Southwest Detroit. The black people that left Detroit only moved slightly north, into mostly white suburbs, and the city at large is still more than 80 percent black. Although you might have read a few things in advance about the city's gentrifying areas getting whiter, those stories don't point out that those areas are still majority black (or that black people can qualify as gentrifiers as well). Greater downtown is 69% black.

It is true that white people are moving into downtown and Midtown neighborhoods just as fast as black residents are leaving neighborhoods in other parts of the city. But if you are white and are planning to move to Detroit, or live here for any point of time, get ready to be stared at. Whites may be gawked at, side-eyed, and maybe questioned about their reason for being in the area in some parts of town.

So what to do? Learn the history of blacks being displaced, "fleed" from, discriminated against, gentrified out, and talked over by whites. Learn how to listen and talk to your neighbors. Then you will better understand the suspicion and resistance you might encounter.

For instance, I live in a neighborhood that was mostly Jewish until the 1960s. One day a tour bus came down my street and parked. Piles of old Jewish women came out of the bus, walking up and down the street snapping photos. This used to be their neighborhood, but clearly not anymore. They weren't afraid of anything, let's be clear. But many of my neighbors stood on their porches on guard, some confused, some ready to strike.

I had a neighbor who is retired, and she kept track of the cars that come in and out of the neighborhood. "I know they're coming, because they're starting to come up and down here," she'll say. By "they," she means white people. She is afraid that our neighborhood will be taken over.

If you are white and new to Detroit and are treated with suspicion, you may cry about it on social media, or speak about it in lowered tones over drinks. You may consult Your Black Friend as to why it seems people just don't like you. But it's not that they don't like you, it's just that we black folks have had so much taken away from us—not just in Detroit, but also in America—that we have to be protective of what little we have.

Basic American history is that blacks were brought here against their will and used as free labor for hundreds of years. There is deeply entrenched distrust of white people among us. As I write this, black Americans are under siege by the police, with seemingly a new death at the hands of law enforcement each week. It has always been tense for black people in America, but these times seem especially uneasy. Here in Detroit, we have those worries—especially when we drive to the suburbs—on top of other concerns.

## THE LOSS OF BLACK BOTTOM AND PARADISE VALLEY

There were once two adjoining neighborhoods in Detroit called Black Bottom and Paradise Valley, both predominantly black. They are both on the lower east side of Detroit, stretching from the edge of downtown and heading northwest on Woodward Avenue toward the Hamtramck border. Black Bottom was named for the rich soil in the land, and Paradise Valley for its burgeoning entertainment scene. They were in the North End section of Detroit, though the borders of North End now are not the same as North End back then.

Every black person of a certain age has a story from Black Bottom, Paradise Valley, or the old North End. My great-grandmother and her three children—my grandfather and two great-aunts—arrived in Detroit by train from Pickens County, Alabama, and settled in a home on Custer Street. My grandfather went to Northern High School, where he played basketball, chartered the school's first National Honor Society, and was a hall monitor. There were two doo-wop singers at Northern High that my grandfather would have to reprimand for singing in the hallways. Those two singers would later pair up with two other singers from Pershing High—which my grandmother attended—and form the Four Tops. My grandfather also tells the story about how a young Smokey Robinson—allegedly—used to rob people at knifepoint long before becoming Motown's greatest songwriter. Hell, everybody in the North End used to run in a tough crowd, even my degreed grandfather. His crew included a man who my great-grandmother thought was always smiling. He was "smiling"

## PARADISE VALLEY AND BLACK BOTTOM

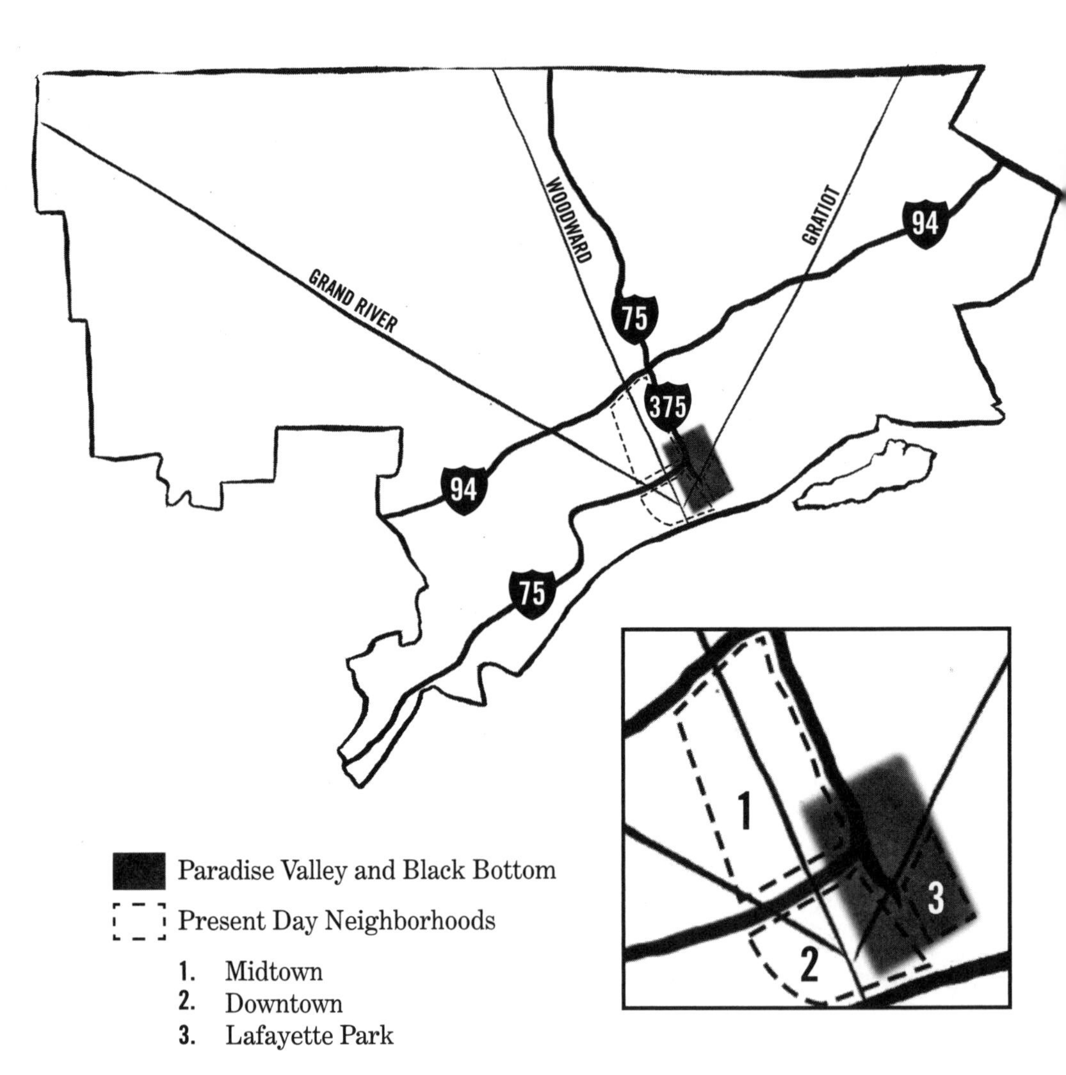

because he lost his upper lip in a knife fight.

Black Bottom was residential, while Paradise Valley was commercial. While Poles crowded into Hamtramck, Jews took up the northwest, and Mexicans the southwest, black residents built an entire entertainment district here—John R, Beaubien, Madison, Vernor, Gratiot, and Brush streets were home to some of the area's most popular businesses.

There was the Gotham Hotel, revered by Langston Hughes as a "minor miracle...Negroes own and manage the Hotel Gotham. If this can happen in Detroit, it can happen elsewhere." Jazz, blues, and burlesque acts of the day—including Ella Fitzgerald, Sarah Vaughn, and Charlie Parker—played at the Flame Show Bar, the 606 Horseshoe Lounge, the Tropicana, Club 666, and elsewhere. Ed Davis, the first black man in Detroit to own a car dealership, had an office on Vernor Highway. Joe Louis, the world-champion boxer, hails from here. So does Robert Hayden, the first black poet laureate.

Factory workers flooding Detroit from the South found homes in Black Bottom and entertained themselves at Paradise Valley in the off-hours. There was symbiosis between the two areas, but poor living conditions and discrimination in employment and housing led to Black Bottom deteriorating almost as fast as it rose. Race riots in 1943 only exacerbated tension in the community, leaving business owners distraught and middle-class residents fleeing.

Stories from the North End are being increasingly lost because much of the current recollection of those neighborhoods is tied to its destruction. Paradise Valley was destroyed when Hastings Street, the main corridor of the entertainment district, was replaced with the Chrysler Freeway, beginning in the late 1950s. The remains of Black Bottom were gone when the Lodge Freeway cut through the other end of the neighborhood, also in the 1950s. The 1967 riots were the final nails in the coffin for both areas.

The goal of redevelopment in those areas, at least on paper, was to foster better living conditions for those who lived there. But poorer black residents were displaced, and prosperous business owners never recovered. The effects of the destruction of Black Bottom and Paradise Valley still linger in Detroit, and are a constant reminder for black residents. If there's ever a reason why someone might be skeptical about new development in Detroit that threatens a long-term resident—and there's a reason why old-timers still refer to the Chrysler and Lodge freeways as "negro removal"—this is why.

## SEGREGATION IN THE 1960S

If you ever wonder why there might be deep distrust among black residents toward white residents, it's because many of us know this history. And because we have more personal stories of discrimination as well.

I was blessed to have two great-grandmothers for the majority of my life but I missed out on having a third.

My grandmother on my mom's side was the third-youngest of eight children. The eight siblings and my great-grandparents moved to a home in Conant Gardens.

Conant Gardens is famous in Detroit for two things: it is the neighborhood that J Dilla, the legendary hip-hop producer, called home, and it is one of the first of the better east-side neighborhoods to which black families started to move. At the time, Detroit was still heavily segregated.

My great-grandmother suffered a heart attack in the family home. One of the siblings dialed for an ambulance. When the ambulance arrived, the two white paramedics who responded said they couldn't take my great-grandmother to the hospital. They didn't know black people had started moving into the neighborhood, and my family would have to find a way to get her to the colored hospital.

By the time they got her there, it was too late. She had died. My great-grandfather moved to Seattle and took up with a second wife. Of the eight siblings, only my grandmother kept in touch with him, sparsely.

One by one, the siblings went along different paths. They all stayed in Detroit, or at least in nearby suburbs. Everyone always wonders what could have been if great-grandmother had lived. Despite all the siblings and their families living in the general area, we're not nearly as close as we should be. We've never had a proper family reunion, unless you count the funerals.

And why did great-grandfather leave? Was he distraught over the treatment of his wife, or was he free from something else? Seattle is as far as you can get from Detroit. I always wonder what he chose to leave behind.

Detroit had segregated hospitals well into the 1960s. Even though Conant Gardens was becoming blacker, other neighborhoods were still off limits back then. Consider the history of how black people have always been treated.

## THE SUBURBS AND SCHOOL CHOICE

Even middle-class and wealthy blacks had a tough time in the older, more racist Detroit.

*Grosse Pointe, Michigan: Race Against Race*, by Kathy Cosseboom, is a must-read for newcomers. It deals in life in the tony Grosse Pointe suburbs northeast of Detroit around the time of the 1967 riots.

The Pointes had a "point system" that real estate agents used for potential homeowners. Applicants were rated based on how "American" they were, their appearance, whether they spoke with an accent, and other identifying characteristics. Obviously, "Negroes and Orientals" ranked at the bottom of the point system.

One lucky black family did make their way to the Pointes, but they were harassed incessantly by their white neighbors. "Nigger, go back down south," one man shouted at the family patriarch driving by.

There are plenty of black folks in the Grosse Pointes now. But 1967 wasn't that long ago, and prejudice is passed down through generations. And it wasn't just Grosse Pointe. Many suburbs had subtle or blatant policies to keep black Detroiters out. In 1940, Ferndale, the now-trendy young-people magnet that everyone loves, erected an eight-foot-high brick wall to keep out blacks. The one black family that did manage to buy a house there was chased away by the Ku Klux Klan.

Fast-forward to today, when black families are leaving Detroit regardless of economic standing. East Detroit Public Schools, the public school system of Eastpointe, an inner-ring east-side suburb, was among the last districts in Metro Detroit to become a district of choice, meaning that a student didn't have to live inside the residential boundary of the district to attend; they had their "choice" of attending those schools or attending the schools of the district where they actually lived. Some East Detroit school board members fought hard against becoming a district of choice because they had already seen "renters" moving in from Detroit and "lowering test scores" when their students entered the district. It was a nice, PC way of saying black people were fucking things up—except no one had actually mentioned race until one meeting, where one board member, a white man whose son also served on the board, said there would be "white flight" from Eastpointe if the district opened its doors.

That board member was forced off the board after those comments. The East Detroit district went choice anyway, and it's more integrated than ever.

## CORKTOWN AND GLOATING OVER FIXING UP A HOUSE

In 2013, someone sprayed anti-gentrification graffiti on an abandoned building near Michigan Central Station. It read "No more homogenization in Southwest" and the word "hipsters" was circled with a red line through it.

Neal Rubin, a columnist for the *Detroit News*, interviewed residents in Corktown and Mexicantown, which sit on opposite sides of the train station, about the graffiti. Both areas were seeing upticks in young white residents; whether you could label the newcomers "hipsters" is up for debate.

One of Rubin's interviewees was a waiter at Mercury Burger Bar, a trendy diner that had opened on the corner of Michigan Avenue and 14th Street. The waiter was also a neighborhood resident, and Rubin's idea of a hipster because he had "nose hoops and ear studs." "If anything, we're helping," he reportedly said. "I feel like we're the ones leading the renovations and getting things done."

The waiter's comments were not received with gratitude by many veteran Southwest and Corktown residents. They read them as smug and condescending.

When does "helping" come off as smug? Easy. When you treat a house renovation, a business opening, or some other good deed as a favor to the people around you rather than simply as a good deed. You should not expect people to bow down to you because you painted the outside of your house.

White people don't often like to hear this, but since many have been so rewarded all their lives for basic accomplishments they're shocked when they're not recognized for something that most people do every day. Millennial whites can be especially insufferable, having grown up in a culture in which everyone gets a trophy just for showing up.

So, we've got a lot of these new whites coming into Detroit with an enormous sense of entitlement and no idea how to react when rose petals aren't strewn at their feet in welcome. Often their reaction is to whine. It's like Yelp reviews in real time: "My neighbors aren't respective of my efforts to save this neighborhood. If it weren't for the walking distance to Café Con Leche, I'd give this one star."

There was a group of new Corktown residents some years ago that called themselves the "Corktown Conquistadors." It was allegedly organized as a "neighborhood improvement group," but some of the neighborhood's older residents bristled at the conquistador term. Were they serious? New residents, coming to conquer and rule over the old? One of the primary goals of the Conquistadors was to shut down a soup kitchen that they argued contributed to "malcontent" in the neighborhood. In other words, they wanted to drive the poor people out. That's what "Old Detroiters" have to deal with: conquistadors who want to mold places into their own likenesses.

I once heard a woman who lived in Southwest Detroit tell a story about a new, young white couple that had moved into the neighborhood. When they moved in, they kept to themselves and didn't speak to any of the Mexicans living on the block. The couple always had friends over, and would often host parties without informing the neighbors. None of the party guests interacted with the neighbors, either.

Don't be that white person. Talk to your neighbors. Leave your savior complex at your parents' house. And if you're going to gentrify, could you at least try to be a little less obnoxious about it?

## HOW TO TALK TO PEOPLE OF COLOR

It's absolutely baffling to me that there are adult white people who don't know how to talk to people of color.

It's the little things. You know how you want to say "black" but say "African-American" instead, and when you do it, you hesitate a little bit, lean in, and say it in a lower tone? Yeah, that. Please don't do that. You won't offend me if you say "black."

A lot of you just smile and give a half-assed wave and think that's enough. How about opening your mouth and saying "hello"? You'd be surprised how far that can go, especially if you're moving into an unfamiliar neighborhood.

It's really simple. Treat others as you'd like to be treated. Say hello. Engage in conversation. We are human beings, not aliens. Don't be afraid to talk to us. We do all the same mundane things you do, like make awkward small talk about the weather followed by a lame joke. What makes you think you are different?

But then there are some white people who like to take things too far. Certainly Americans of color could use more allies (although the term "ally" can be troubling, as if it's something that you can opt out of if the going gets too rough). All at once, some of Detroit's new white people are crusaders, race-relations experts, civil rights leaders, and peace activists, taking up for the cause and going out of their way to show how much they're "down" with us.

But let's dial it down a notch when the situation doesn't call for a race-relations forum.

I once spoke with a few other panelists to a group of local mid-career executives who wanted to help push Detroit forward, but were unsure about how to get around some of the racial barriers here. There was a young white panelist who talked on and on and on about the struggles of black Detroiters and how more white people should let black people have a voice in their own city. And he talked so damn much I couldn't get a word in myself. So thanks a lot, social justice white guy, for being the voice of black Detroit. What would we ever do without you?

Know that if you lean toward the progressive side of things that not everything in Detroit is cause for reaction. Are you happy that you're living in a diverse neighborhood and everyone's getting along? Great! Don't be so proud of yourself for doing what people do every day. Are you upset that a certain population of Detroit seems to be maligned in some way? That's fine, you should be. But be aware that sometimes your silence can allow others to be heard.

And did you know that some of us black people do not want to talk about race all the time? I can't tell you how many times I've sat down with people and the conversation always descends into something about black people in Detroit. Talking about race can be complicated and exhausting, because most of the time white people are asking us to speak on behalf of entire communities. (Hint: We can't. We all have different experiences, we all have different Detroit experiences. It can't be stressed enough, especially here in Detroit, that we have *similar* experiences but we are not a monolith.)

It's not that we can't talk about it; choosing not to talk about it would be choosing to ignore what makes us who we are. But can't we talk about something else sometimes? How about those Tigers, huh?

---

So you've read all this and you've decided that you're one of those white people that "doesn't see race" or you're one of those obtuse white people who complain on the internet about black people not being able to function in society despite slavery ending years ago. Well, you're probably going to be miserable in Detroit. You're going to be that person who reads the dailies and sees a murder in Detroit and wonders why "the black community" doesn't just get itself together. You're the person that will only share stories about crimes committed by black criminals, simply to confirm what you think is true about black people everywhere. You'll probably end up living in the suburbs eventually, but not just any suburb—you'll end up way out in Macomb County, chasing developers to see how high the mile road system can go. Detroit won't be the place for you.

But if you have read all this and want to learn even more about the history of the city and don't consider yourself a savior, well then you will do fine here. Welcome to Detroit. Don't forget to pay your property taxes.

*You went to*
**CRANBROOK,**
*that's a private school!*

—B-Rabbit, *8 Mile*

# CHAPTER 7

## HOW TO MAKE PEACE WITH THE SUBURBS

One of the first people you meet upon moving to Detroit will be an overenthusiastic native of Detroit's suburbs who can't wait to tell you how awful the suburbs are. We'll call them Madonnas.

You know, Madonna the pop star. She was born Madonna Lourdes Ciccone, and raised in Bay City, a city two hours north of Detroit, and Rochester Hills, an actual suburb of Detroit. She graduated from Adams High School, went to the University of Michigan for a time, dropped out, moved to New York, and never looked back.

It is written in the unofficial Detroit rulebook that anyone with even the most tenuous connection to the city must hold it up high at every opportunity. When pursuing solo stardom after leaving the Supremes, Diana Ross would ask her relatives at home in Detroit to watch over her children, believing that life in the inner city would keep her wealthy offspring guarded. At the height of her career, Anita Baker filmed a music video in Detroit, paying tribute to the many landmarks she frequented prior to becoming a force. She lives in the Detroit suburbs today, as do Aretha Franklin, Bob Seger, and Eminem.

In her 30-year-long career, Madonna has toured many times, but has not stopped in Detroit on a few of her outings. She has negative things to say of her upbringing in Rochester Hills, calling it boring and uncultured. But, unlike Madonna, most of those who find the suburbs beige don't make it to New York City and superstardom.

They just come right down I-96 or I-75 and plop themselves in the mix in Detroit. And they won't shut the fuck up for two seconds about how uneventful their lives were in the 'burbs. They are Madonnas.

---

One of my mother's best friends used to have a condo in Southfield in a high-rise tower. I watched *Little Man Tate* on a big TV there, in a living room with tall windows from which you could barely see the Detroit skyline miles away.

This condo was the piece of the pie the Jeffersons were taking about. Southfield was for years an inner-ring suburb to which well-to-do African-Americans moved on up. There was a time, for a lot of us, when it signaled that you made it.

In the 1980s and 90s a lot of Detroit blacks started to head north. Crack was spreading through the city like kudzu, Devil's Night fires were at an all-time high. Not every neighborhood plunged into the abyss; the neighborhood I grew up in still stands today, even though we had a local crackhead who stole our snowblower in the summer and our lawnmower in the winter. But for those who could afford to move up, leaving Detroit when things were getting bad – but not nearly as bad as the economic collapse of the late 2000s – was simply a preemptive strike.

In Detroit, blacks tend to follow Jews to the city limits. Southfield, as well as a few Oakland County suburbs, had seen meteoric rises in Jewish populations in the years since the 1967 riots In the 1980s, Southfield's black population began to swell as well. Hope United Methodist Church was one of the epicenters of the new Southfield, as well as a general galvanizer of suburban black Detroit.

Hope was a struggling Methodist church with a declining white congregation. A new pastor was installed, but congregants were shocked to discover that the governing body had chosen a black minister. Some of the congregation did not take it well. Despite his credentials—the new pastor was the fourth in a line of Methodist preachers —he was often served coffee with coagulated saliva frothing atop the cup. But if you've read the Bible, it's full of stories about testing the worthy and the chosen.

White congregants began leaving the church in droves, but as word of a new, fiery preacher began spreading, new black families poured in, including mine. When we formally became members of Hope, only one white family remained. They always looked so out of place. It was a married couple with four or five children, dressed so dowdy and dull. Us blacks show *up*! and show *out*! for the Lord: big church hats, sequins, glitter, furs, gator shoes, gold bracelets. Still, whenever the congregation rose for a hymn, the white family rose as well. They sang along to the black hymns, and always stood in line to thank the pastor after service.

How strange was it that the only white family in the church seemed to be the least prejudiced? The thing about black families in the suburbs was that they bred a whole generation of snobby-ass kids. Not bourgeois. Beyond bourgeois. Just straight-up noveau riche wannabes with little connection to their parents' home cities and a warped sense of reality.

Hope had a youth church that my mom made me go to, and in that youth church were two black girls who went to West Bloomfield High School. Despite being black in the Midwest, they both had Valley Girl accents, using our down times during service to talk about their mall escapades, their all-night parties, and who's-dating-who in what-clique. Picture Dionne in *Clueless*, only twice as haughty, and not nearly as in touch with their own culture as they should have. Dionne at least knew the importance of black hair maintenance. Based on how dry these girls' hair was, they were obviously taking tips from their white classmates.

One day the youth pastor asked about *Jubilee*, a novel about slavery, and whether any of us were familiar with it. "Oh, no," one of the West Bloomfield girls replied. "That's Detroit Public Schools."

Public. I can never forget the icy chill in her voice when she said that word. It's like—you go to a public school, too! But a public school in the suburbs is just so much better than a Detroit one, right?

I didn't say anything then, but I should have. Maybe God took care of her for me.

---

Ask any suburban Detroit resident what they associate with their hometown and you'll likely get a variety of answers, most of them negative.

Small-minded. Racist. Subdivisions. Meth addicts. Heroin addicts. Hicks. "Everyone from my high school still lives there." Backwards. Conservative. They are ashamed of where they are from.

Around the holidays, your suburban-born friends who now live in the city lament having to drive all the way up (insert freeway here) for the holidays, because suburbia is so lame. Never mind that their car insurance may be registered there. But it's just such an inconvenience to drive a few miles away from Detroit.

Something to keep in mind when living in Detroit is to stop fucking complaining about the suburbs after you move here. I get it, some of you might have had parents and grandparents that were part of the resistance to anything having to do with Detroit. But some of you still had comfortable upbringings not always seen here in the city.

I grew up in a fairly safe middle-class enclave of the city. Not all Detroiters did. I remember a girl in my high school talking about the street she lived on: "Abandoned house, abandoned house, regular house, abandoned house..." *Why can't she just move?* I used to think. But even before the economic crash, people couldn't. Be grateful that your parents' cookie-cutter colonial isn't surrounded by blight.

---

Regardless of what suburb you grew up in or what suburb you may choose to live in now, you must identify yourself as being from that suburb when you go out of town. That's the rule, sorry. You are not from Detroit if you grew up in Shelby Township.

Detroiters are territorial. We are territorial because we have our own culture here that is not duplicated elsewhere—and I'm not talking about coney dogs. I'm talking about dancing, music, architecture, fashion, slang, attitudes. There may not be much difference between someone who grew up in, say, Sylvania Township and someone who grew up in Toledo. But there are huge differences between people who grew up in the city limits of Detroit versus the suburbs.

Now for the record, we're all from Metro Detroit. But there's still a difference between *Detroit* and *Metro Detroit*. Generally speaking, Metro Detroit is the tri-county area that includes Wayne County, Oakland County, and Macomb County. Detroit is obviously the anchor. It's in Wayne County.

The Wikipedia mafia will be quick to point out that certain census designations include other counties like Washtenaw, Lapeer, St. Clair, Livingston, and Monroe. But if we're talking cultural similarities, driving distances, and the evolution of the city and its suburbs, the tri-county definition is the way to go.

Like a lot of things around here, these divisions are tied to the race and class divisions that were established decades ago. If someone's from Highland Park, Texas, they're going to say they're from Dallas. If someone's from Highland Park, Michigan, they're going to say they're from Highland Park.

It's not as easy to say "I'm from Detroit" when so many politicians and residents over the years have done all they could to disassociate themselves from the city. And as I've pointed out several times here, Detroiters themselves have an odd complex about identifying themselves that's a mix of city pride and stubborn resistance.

*L. Brooks Patterson*

An easy example to point to is Oakland County Executive L. Brooks Patterson, who for years has trashed Detroit in favor of protecting the (very white, very wealthy) Oakland County. Even though there are parts of Oakland County that aren't so white and wealthy. Like Pontiac! So no one from Oakland County is going to say they're from Oakland County, or Detroit. They're going to tell you exactly what their address is.

Another example is Eastpointe, a small city in Macomb County. Years ago, the city was known as East Detroit (despite the fact that it's geographically north of Detroit). The city changed its name to Eastpointe to associate itself with the wealthy Grosse Pointe suburbs (although neither East Detroit nor its current incarnation were ever wealthy), thus removing all trace of "Detroit" from its history—except the schools, because the high school alumni association wanted to preserve the name of where they graduated from. It's that sort of mentality—"I'm not from Detroit, I'm from _____"—that runs deep here.

---

There's a good chance you will end up living in the suburbs—and that is totally fine. No really—no sarcasm here. It is okay to not live in the city limits, for a variety of legitimate reasons.

For one, because the region is so huge and has developed at different times, you can find a wide variety of architecture not readily available in your favorite Detroit neighborhood. Southfield and Lathrup Village, for example, are full of midcentury ranches perfect for fans of that era. The Grosse Pointes are lined with English Tudors that envy the ones in west-side Detroit. Cities along lakes big and small, like Wyandotte, St. Clair Shores, Sylvan Lake, or Keego Harbor, have homes overlooking beautiful bodies of water.

There are also conveniences not offered in the city. Say what you will about the optimism in resurgent Detroit, but walkable neighborhoods—the kind where you can walk a few blocks and suddenly there are Starbucks's and tapas joints – are in shorter supply. Many of Metro Detroit's smaller cities—like Plymouth, a Wayne County town close to Ann Arbor—have well-developed downtowns in close proximity to residential neighborhoods. Some larger suburbs have busy corridors stocked with strip malls, if that's your thing. And if that is your thing, don't feel ashamed.

But the main reason why someone might move to the suburbs is children. If you've got kids, you're going to have to put them in school. And right now, Detroit schools aren't the best for anyone, including existing residents. When it comes to choosing between your child's education or cheap rent in your studio/living space where the closest school has children not passing the statewide test because the whole system is totally unprepared to deal with a rapidly declining population, I'd probably go with your kids' well-being.

Whatever you do, though, don't be a Madonna. The suburbs have issues and not everyone who lives there is perfect. But to not be a Detroit jackass is to realize that this entire region is divided, and one of the only ways for the city to progress is if this whole area works together. Sounds cliché, but I'm only repeating what local leaders are finally starting to realize. Cranky old Patterson is going to kick the bucket one day, meaning Oakland County won't be as toxic. He'll probably go down hating Detroit like he does now, but other county executives around him are realizing the benefits of co-existence.

## FORTY WAYS TO TELL IF YOU'RE NEW DETROIT:

1. You take "bankruptcy selfies" with the legal folks who steered the city through municipal bankruptcy.

2. The only high school you can name is Cass Tech.

3. You complain about the Woodward Dream Cruise.

4. You own at least four of the following T-shirts: "Detroit Hustles Harder," the "D-E-T-R-O-I-T" shift gate pattern, "Detroit Vs. Everybody," "Made in Detroit," "Detroit: Where the Weak Are Killed and Eaten," "Detroit" (in the shape of a pistol), "Say Nice Things About Detroit ..." but have never heard of Marc Buchanan or Tracy Reese.

5. Parking tickets make you irrationally angry.

6. You argue about which of Detroit's newest restaurants have the best fried chicken.

7. Getting your bike stolen means you're "officially a real Detroiter."

8. You use the term "real Detroiter."

9. The most dramatic thing to happen to you this week is a disagreement in your neighborhood's private Facebook group.

10. A Detroit flag is hanging outside your front door.

11. Your pool of dateable 30-something white residents is getting shallow.

12. You're confident that your recently published guest column is exactly what Detroit needs to hear right now.

13. "My mom was born in Hutzel Hospital" is your comeback.

14. You want your child to experience as much Detroit culture as possible, so you bring them to microbreweries and gastropubs.

15. You wonder why Detroit is such a food desert and why there aren't more healthy eateries, though you regularly engage in raucous "Lafayette vs. American" debates online.

16. Lafayette and American are the only two coney islands in the city you've ever frequented.

17. You've used the word "vibrant" to describe your neighborhood.

18. Getting tweeted by a local journalist excites you.

19. You've felt a sense of accomplishment by using the "See, Click, Fix" app.

20. You have at least three home décor items made of reclaimed wood.

21. You've bragged about going to a "ghetto chicken place."

22. When people ask why you moved here, the only answer you give is "cheap rent."

23. You believe an app can help people stave off foreclosure.

24. You remember the good ol' days when Marche du Nain Rouge wasn't mainstream.

25. You have a super cool idea for the train station and why won't Matty Moroun just listen?

26. The only articles you share on social media are the positive ones.

27. Getting a membership at the Detroit Athletic Club and the Detroit Yacht Club is on your bucket list.

28. Your first thought upon hearing of a major road or freeway project concerns the bike lanes.

29. You moved to Detroit in 2013 and you argue with people who moved to Detroit in 2014.

30. A place you're visiting "doesn't have enough Motown influence."

31. You consider any area with more than two ethnic groups a version of Hamtramck.

32. You hear about a chain restaurant opening and you're concerned about Detroit losing its authenticity.

33. You think you know exactly what the "average Detroiter" expects in retail, food and other establishments.

34. You use terms like "average Detroiter."

35. You have a "Made in Detroit" bumper sticker on the back of your Fiat.

36. Tweeting about 313 Day really brings out that sense of pride.

37. Development in Pontiac upsets you.

38. The question "why can't Detroit just absorb Highland Park" has crossed your lips.

39. If "Belle Isle suddenly feels more safer."

40. Your first thought upon making a friend who is not the same race as you is to blog about it.

**MAN**

*instead of being the end, becomes the mere means—*

**A TOOL OF PRODUCTION.**

*He is a cost to be eliminated the moment there is no need for his services…*

**[WE] DEMAND FOR A PROPER SCALE OF** *moral values* **WHICH PUTS PEOPLE ABOVE PROPERTY, MEN ABOVE MACHINES.**

—Walter Reuther, labor union leader

# CHAPTER 8

## HOW TO DRIVE IN DETROIT

Kids in Detroit are taught to hustle as early as elementary school. There is a company in metro Detroit called Morley Candy Company. The candy company offers schools across the state, but especially in Detroit, opportunities for fundraisers by selling chocolate bars, truffles, summer sausage, and other seasonal edibles. When a school participates in the program, each child is handed a catalogue, an order form, and a due date to by which to sell as much of the shit as possible, because Detroit Public Schools always needs money for something.

When I was growing up, winners were incentivized with gifts based on how much they sell. Sell within the lowest threshold, and you might get a fanny pack. Even higher thresholds netted gifts like cassette players or autographed sports memorabilia. The goal of the fundraisers, aside from funding a pizza party or some other special program, was to teach children salesmanship and self-confidence. Half of the time, though, this wasn't the case since we simply handed the form to our parents to do the dirty work for us. The other half led to awkward encounters with fellow students; one year, a girl in my class who lived in my apartment complex knocked on our door, order form and catalogue in hand. What were we going to do, buy from each other?

I went to Walter P. Chrysler Elementary School, just a few blocks from the Walter P. Chrysler Freeway. Both are named for the founder of Chrysler Corporation. And because our school was (and still is) on the east side of Detroit, a lot of parents of students worked for Chrysler—which had and still has plants on that side of town—in some capacity, particularly in the auto plants. I remember being jealous of one girl because her father, a Chrysler employee, had a brand new Chrysler Concorde. The Concorde was built on Chrysler's LH platform, an innovation described by automotive industry insiders as Chrysler's "last hope" before sliding into bankruptcy in the 1990s. My mother yearned for a Dodge Intrepid, which was the exact same car as the Concorde with a different badge and sportier trim.

At Chrysler Elementary, the top three candy sellers got special prizes from the school in addition to whatever Morley handed us. And those top three students always had parents working in the plants. Their parents simply handed their order forms down the assembly line and let the magic work itself. Despite fears of Chrysler going under—it had just swallowed the remains of American Motor Company, the last of the American automakers from Detroit's golden age, and was relying on AMC's Jeep brand and platforms to bring in new customers—a healthy number of Detroiters worked there, as well as at General Motors and Ford, well into the 2000s. And everyone knew someone who did.

The influence of the American auto industry is not only seen in schools and highways named after its forebears, but in the way Detroiters, for a long time, interacted on a daily basis. There are men and women whose entire wardrobes, save for church wear, are comprised of United Auto Workers paraphernalia, their union numbers adorning varsity-style jackets, sweatshirts, windbreakers, and key chains. Whenever someone wants to buy a new car, they immediately hit up an auto-worker relative for a family discount. You could always get a job at the plant when there were no other options. All three automakers threw money toward community service projects, children's programs, church dinners—you could not go to an event without seeing someone's logo on the program or a T-shirt.

Two misconceptions among newcomers, though, are that everyone works in the auto industry—I mean, people think no one wants anything more than to build cars—and that everyone drives American. My parents did not work in the industry, though my mom's side of the family was drawn here from the South to work in the plants, and my dad's dad is a Ford retiree. But everyone does know someone connected, even tangentially, in the industry. Driving American, though, how do I explain this? Well…

---

Ever heard of Vincent Chin? Vincent Chin was a 27-year-old Chinese-American man from the Detroit suburb of Oak Park celebrating his last days of bachelorhood out on the town at a strip club in Highland Park (incidentally, where Chrysler Corporation was headquartered for several years before moving into Oakland County) in 1982.

Here's what was going on in the automotive world in 1982. The American car companies had spent years making large, gas-guzzling sedans and too-sporty muscle cars, neglecting changing consumer attitudes toward smaller vehicles and fuel efficiency. And despite the assembly lines in Detroit and other car towns backboning the middle class in America, Asian carmakers proved far more efficient at building affordable automobiles. Japanese companies, with spiffy compacts like the Toyota Corolla and Honda Civic, began increasing market share during this time, just as the country entered into a recession.

All this spelled trouble for the Detroit companies, and Chrysler was the first to wave the white flag. The company received more than a billion dollars in government loans—we call those "bailouts" now—but still had to cut costs. That meant layoffs at plants. Ronald Ebens, a manager at a Chrysler truck plant in Warren, a Macomb County suburb just north of the Eight Mile border on the east side, was one of those laid off.

Ebens and his stepson, Michael Nitz, happened to cross paths with Chin at the strip club on that awful June night. They exchanged words – no one is quite clear how exactly the exchange began—and began fighting in the club. The indoor fight died down; it re-escalated outdoors. It ended with Ebens using a baseball bat to club Chin to death outside a nearby McDonald's while Nitz held him down. Eyewitnesses say Ebens said to Chin that "it's because of you motherfuckers" that he and other Chrysler workers had been laid off. It doesn't take a genius to figure out what Ebens meant when he said that, even if they didn't know Chin was Chinese and Japanese automakers were what was causing Detroit's woes.

Ebens and Nitz initially faced murder charges, but got off relatively scot-free with manslaughter convictions, probation, and heavy fines paid to Chin's family. They served no jail time. Chin's death spurred angry protests in Detroit's Asian-American community and nationwide, but while Ebens was later convicted on a federal charge of violating Chin's civil rights, that conviction was overturned on appeal. Eventually, the story faded from public consciousness and was filed away as just another Motor City tragedy. It's not widely taught in grade school; I learned about Chin in college by chance, covering an Asian student organization's event for my college paper.

What didn't stop after Chin's death was the growing market share of Asian automakers in the States, or the anti-Asian sentiment geared toward foreign industry. When you move to Detroit, you'll have to keep your outrage at bay if you are trailing an F-150 with a bumper sticker that reads: "My truck is made of steel, not chopsticks."

There hasn't been a moment in history where Americans weren't hostile to immigrants, foreigners, whatever your term of choice may be. Detroit, despite being a city of immigrants, was no different. Nowadays, we've grown more politically correct in referring to Toyotas and Nissans as "imports" rather than "foreign cars." But don't be surprised if you run across the latter term, in a delivery dripping with contempt.

Consider, however, that pride in American workmanship far predates the Chin killing. Listen to all those old rock 'n' roll songs of the 1950s. Are they singing about Volkswagens? No, those songs are all about American steel and horsepower, most of which originated right here in Detroit.

---

My mother's first car was a Ford Granada. She later drove a Ford Mustang, and then a Ford Tempo. I learned to drive on my grandmother's Mercury Lynx, the sister car to the Ford Escort, and my first car was a Ford Focus. My grandparents on my mom's side have owned every generation Ford Explorer and regularly lease Lincolns. Because my grandfather on my dad's side is a Ford retiree, almost everyone on that side of my family drives a Ford.

It didn't mean that I never knew anyone to drive an import. One of the first automotive terms I learned as a toddler was "lift-back," the term Toyota used on the early-'80s Celica driven by my stylish cousin. My mom's best friend from college drove a Nissan Sentra with a bad muffler. My other cousin's first car was a Honda Accord with flip-up headlights, a stick shift, and a modified sound system to showcase his 1990s rap. His mother, my grandfather's sister, drove a Mazda 323. My grandfather's other sister drove an ocean-blue Volkswagen Beetle, her beloved Bug.

I played with Hot Wheels, Matchbox, and Majorette cars growing up. My favorites were a white Mercury Sable station wagon, a maroon Saab 9000, and a Mercedes-Benz 300E. That's one American, one Swede, and one German. There was a time when I wanted my first car to be a Hyundai Scoupe, but my grandfather promised me a Mustang when I turned 16. (I never got it.)

I wasn't really beat over the head with "buy American," but I was born during a time of shifting attitudes toward imports. Mercedes-Benz, Jaguar, and BMW were seen as aspirational – something higher than Cadillac or Lincoln, just to let folks know you've made it. Pick up an old *Jet* magazine, and see how many black celebrities pose next to the hoods of their Mercedes convertibles.

I had a great-aunt who was head of nursing at a Detroit hospital who drove Corollas from the 1970s until she died in 1991. Her son drove a Volkswagen Golf, while her two daughters drove American: a Corvette for the older one, a Buick Century for the younger. Cars like Corollas and Golfs were seen as thrifty, budget-saving options, a welcome choice for many locals who wanted to save a dime or two.

Then there was Hyundai. Everyone knows that if you have bad credit or hardly any kind of down payment, you go find a Hyundai dealership. Or Mitsubishi. They give their cars away! (Remember, poverty rates, unequal wages, and other financial calamities have haunted many black Americans for generations. Detroiters are no different.) Then Kia came along, and it seemed like every model they had was under 10 grand. I lived next door to a preacher and his wife who had 10 children in a three-bedroom house. The oldest daughter was able to save up enough to buy a Kia Rio, which sold for around $7,000 out the door at the time.

There are myriad reasons why someone might drive an import in Detroit, but I can tell you this about everyone I've known to drive foreign: they've never had their tires slashed. They've never gotten into a fight with someone that works at one of the plants. They've never been refused service by a mechanic. Never had anything spray-painted on the hood of their car. Never had their windows busted out, their brakes cut, their car explode when they turn on the ignition.

You may get a snide remark or two if someone sees you in an import. That will be the extent of it. I drove a Honda Civic for a little while, and my dad's dad, the Ford retiree, was a little upset about it. After all, he built Fords, so why couldn't *I* drive what *he* built? I tried to explain that things had changed, and that he retired a long time ago, and that my little Honda purchase wasn't going to bankrupt Ford, and so on and so forth, but he wasn't hearing it. He did not, however, disown me or love me any less.

I eventually bought a Ford Fusion, which is what I drive now. But it was built in Mexico.

---

I loved cars all my life and thought enough of myself to work for a car publication. I spent a year and a half writing for *Ward's*, a trade pub that voraciously covers the innards of the automotive industry.

There are magazines like *Motor Trend* and *Road & Track*, and *Car & Driver*, the ones I grew up reading—they are called "buff books" among car enthusiasts—and then there are publications like *Ward's*, *Automotive News*, and *Detroit Auto Scene*. The former are for gearheads who like to put posters on their walls, soup up their used coupes as much as they can in high school, and later graduate to big-boy muscle cars when they can afford them. The latter are the trade publications that talk about things like impending union strikes, the strength of the Japanese yen, executive management changes, and future product plans. The activities covered by the trades beget the stylish finished products covered in the buff books.

During my time at *Ward's*, we were trying to figure out if a subsidiary of one of the Big Three was nearing the end of its run. Ford had pulled the plug on Mercury and put Volvo up for sale. General Motors had let go of Oldsmobile, Geo, Pontiac, Saturn, and Hummer. Chrysler put Plymouth and Eagle to bed.

But this brand wasn't just any brand, it was Dodge—one of the pillars of Chrysler, a legendary namesake of the Detroit auto industry, and a crucial part of the current industry. The brand itself could not go head-to-head with Toyota or Honda. But it was and still is a large slice of Chrysler's pie, offering key models in key segments that would be missed if the brand were killed.

*Fiat Chrysler CEO Sergio Marchionne and Chrysler commercial star (oh, also rapper) Eminem.*

Automotive suppliers—the people that make seats and turbochargers and infotainment systems and transmissions and other parts of cars—are given directives from automakers about forthcoming product plans, long before the rest of the world knows. And suppliers were hearing things about every Chrysler brand except Dodge.

At the time, Dodge's product plan released to media also seemed vague. While Chrysler had plans for Jeep, Ram, and Fiat, Dodge seemed stagnant with its current lineup. Dodge's lineup was already dwindling as it was; the stalwart pickup trucks were separated from Dodge and spun off unto its own brand, and Chrysler had previously announced that one of the minivans in the stable would be killed off. Rumor had it the Dodge Grand Caravan was going to be that minivan.

We felt confident enough at *Ward's* to print a few stories that basically asked what the hell was going on. It was written in a language that only automotive executives would understand, pointing squarely at the lack of information given to suppliers about the brand lining up with previously disclosed information about Dodge's overall product plan. But those reports were picked up and spun by automotive blogs who basically wrote Dodge's obituary and nailed the coffin shut with their own speculation.

Each summer, Chrysler invites media from around the country and from some foreign countries to an event they call "What's New," at which they show off their entire product line. The amount of money the car companies spend on writers to get them to say nice things about their product—all for the purpose of sending good messages to you, the consumer—is mind-blowing. The flight and lodging costs, plus the expenses of catered food from a top restaurant, and enough fuel to gas up the vehicles at the disposal of speed-demon writers, would make Suze Orman or Clark Howard explode with rage. Regardless, "What's New" is also an opportunity for journalists to talk to executives one on one. By the time "What's New" rolled around that year, the "is Dodge dead?" question was heavy on everyone's mind, but no one had any executive comment. This was the chance for someone to get it.

I cornered one Chrysler executive for a one-on-one interview. Voice recorder in hand, I asked him point-blank about what the plan was for Dodge.

"You're making this shit up about the Dodge brand. Why are you making this shit up about the Dodge brand? You started it!" he told me. "Shit" would be as frequently used in this conversation as "Challenger" and "Durango."

"I don't know why you're making shit up and spraying it all over the market," he continued. "The Dodge brand is the number-one selling brand in the Chrysler group. It's like saying the Ford brand is going away and they're going to start selling Lincolns. It's like saying Chevy is going away and they're going to start selling GMC."

The numbers weren't adding up. I asked him about the Dodge Dart, a compact car that had a huge marketing campaign but hardly had sales to match. The one TV show that's advertised constantly, but doesn't have the Nielsen ratings to match and could be canceled after the first season.

"The Dart is brand new. It hasn't even seen its year birthday yet," he said, hinting that sales would rise in the months to come. They didn't. A few months later, the executive's boss, Chrysler CEO Sergio

Marchionne, would tell a group of reporters at the North American International Auto Show that the Dart's sales "were not as well as I wanted."

But our executive was relentless about Dodge. "I think you should stop making shit up. As far as I'm concerned I'm not even going to talk to you anymore because it's such a waste of my time. I tell you certain things, and then you write something completely different," he said.

Car enthusiasts in Detroit are not to be fucked with. If you don't know the difference between a supercharger and a turbocharger, don't even bother trying to jump into the conversation. If you've never heard those terms in your life, just don't bother at all.

But car executives are a completely different breed of unfuckwithable. They're car enthusiasts with ruling power, sometimes far too much. They've worked their whole lives to get where they are. They could build a car from scratch with their bare hands if they wanted to, but instead they use thousands of laborers to build the cars they've always wanted as adolescents. Visiting journalists write about how Detroiters have motor oil in their veins, but a lot of them don't; they just build the cars and go home. Car executives are the ones who actually eat and shit spark plugs.

I talked to a different Chrysler executive at "What's New" some time later that day. He, too, knew exactly what I was going to ask, but he offered a more sympathetic take. Soon after the "is Dodge dead?" stories started circulating, Chrysler dealers started panicking. Leading dealers began flooding Chrysler's headquarters in Auburn Hills with calls, wondering if their sales staff would be out of a job soon.

There was also concern spreading throughout the company, particularly on factory floors where Dodges were built. Chrysler had gone through layoffs in the 1970s and early 1980s, was near death again in the 1990s, had changed ownership three times in the last decade and a half, and filed bankruptcy in 2009. The death of Dodge could have been the death of Chrysler as a whole.

"Holy shit," I asked myself. "Did I almost kill Dodge?"

---

"You don't need a car in Detroit" is one of the biggest fucking lies I've ever heard.

If you're moving to Detroit and you've heard this, let it go immediately. We don't have New York's subway system or Chicago's el trains or the Bay Area's BART. You could survive without a car, yes. But you will find yourself bumming rides more often than not.

There are places that are not as easily accessible by public transit, cab, or bike. There is no bus that can take you to Detroit Metropolitan Airport, which is not in the city of Detroit. There are no casual bus rides to the Detroit Zoo, which is also not in the city of Detroit. When people say that they don't need a car, what they are really saying is that they hate cars and therefore anyone who has a car is a threat to the bike-riding utopia they are trying to build.

Detroit is going to have a tumultuous relationship with bicycles for a long time, so if you're coming here on two wheels, be prepared. Are people going to purposely run you down with their car because they can't stand the sight of you? Absolutely not—and there are more creative ways to commit murder, anyway! But will there be occasions where a driver may not see you because they're not used to seeing bikes on the road? Yes.

The growing attitude among bike riders is that the city of Detroit should bow down to the cycling community. The city has improved bike infrastructure somewhat; there are bike lanes on many major streets, and the Dequindre Cut, which stretches from Eastern Market to Jefferson Avenue, is a popular greenway for bikers. But there are a few things preventing the city from being as bike-friendly as it could be. The city does not have the resources to install bike lanes on every single street, and the fact that there are more pressing concerns, such as fixing public transportation, than catering to every single city resident who prefers bikes over motors.

Cyclists in Detroit, just like in any city, tend to take out their frustrations on car owners. They wonder aloud why everyone in Detroit can't just give up their cars and join them on the bike parade. For starters, if you've got a family, you can't just give up your minivan and shuttle your kids to school, doctor's appointments, basketball practice, church, and grandma's Sunday dinner on a Schwinn. Next, a significant degree of the population is aging. If you're in your 70s and you've had a few surgeries in your lifetime, riding a bike isn't for you. Then there's safety. I had a neighbor who biked everywhere until he was robbed at gunpoint. Now he walks.

Cyclists in Detroit forget that riding is a privilege that few can afford. Sure, if you happen to live in a safe(r) neighborhood with things close by, it can be a breeze. But those neighborhoods come at a cost many Detroiters can't afford. So when cyclists finally realize this, they turn their aggression toward the automakers.

Let anyone on two wheels tell it, and the Big Three and the Japanese and the Germans and everybody else are all in bed together to keep Detroiters driving cars until all the Earth's roads are drowned from all the ice caps finally melting, upon which time we'll be converted to superpowered autonomous hovercrafts built by the merger of General Motors, Toyota, and Volkswagen. Every car executive is Judge Doom from *Who Framed Roger Rabbit*, apparently.

To not be a jackass in Detroit, you will have to learn to live with the car companies. You are allowed to make fun of Chrysler for having its headquarters in Auburn Hills and being taken over by an Italian automaker. You can wag your finger at Ford for being in Dearborn. Play that suburb vs. city card as much as you'd like, or maybe even the bailout card if you want to be a dick about it, but that's as far as you'll get.

It is complete jackassery to disrespect the Big Three on any other grounds, however. Many people in suburbs tend to become total elitists when talking about people that work there, because they usually point to the ones that graduated high school and went directly to the plants after graduation. They talk about how they "made it" out of Warren, Lake Orion, Flint, Trenton, and other factory towns and how those that were left behind just aren't worthy.

I've spent time in the plants as an automotive reporter. I had relatives that work there. I live in the same neighborhood with them; we all do as Detroiters. If you've spent any amount of time in a plant, or heard any of the stories from the line, you'd know that these are some of the hardest-working motherfuckers on the planet. The men and women in the plants have varied backgrounds. A large amount of them served in the armed forces and many couldn't find work after their service and got their feet in the door of the industry through various veteran feeder programs. There are some, especially as of late, who went to college and couldn't find work in their field, so they wound up on the line. And then there are the many who joined the ranks when all this talk of having a degree was unnecessary, but used their earnings to simply provide for their families—families you might be neighbors with here in Detroit. Their pride for their work knows no bounds. They are no less of a Detroiter than you. Don't piss on the industry that built the town you decided to call home.

---

If I ever get rich, I'm not buying the Mustang my grandfather once promised me. I'm getting a BMW M5.

For the non-automotive enthusiasts, the M5 is a high-powered variant of BMW's midsize 5-Series sedan. In layman's terms, it has a higher-powered engine and a faster 0-60 time. It's not a cushy ride like some of BMW's other vehicles, but it is comfortable for its class. It's not cheap; I test-drove one with a sticker price of more than $100,000. Despite its prowess and good looks, it's still a German car, somewhat of a betrayal of Detroit and the ties to American carmaking my family has.

I'm of two minds of the "buy American" ethos that covers this town. I think that it's a free market, a free country, and you should buy what you want. But I also think you don't buy American, you should, at the very least, *consider* buying American.

If you want to be the die-hard Detroiter, the one that wears Detroit-branded T-shirts every Saturday to Eastern Market, the one who gets excited for Opening Day, the one who wants to have your name up in lights on the Fox Theatre marquee on your wedding day, you should buy American. But for those on the fence, here's some quick advice:

1. If you're moving here or getting settled here in your foreign car, go ahead and keep it. You're welcome almost everywhere, with the rare exception of an American automotive plant, where there are signs instructing owners of foreign cars to park in the lots the furthest away from the main entrances. (Seriously. But you won't be towed or anything.)

2. Respect the industry. Do not try to start a petition or a Facebook page calling for the end of the industry just because you want to ride your bike. Know that there are millions—yes, millions—of

people dependent on the industry, and not just the people who work there. Not just Detroit. Factory towns and the businesses that support them, the schools where their children attend, the numerous suppliers that support the automakers ... there would be catastrophe if the industry folded. Well, actually, there already has been catastrophe. The lingering effects of the industry's falters should be immediately seen when you move here.

3. If you've got a bright idea for an industry that can employ thousands of people in Detroit that's not automotive, let's hear it!

4. Respect the folks in the industry. You don't have to tip your hat or bow down, but if you come across someone, be they on the line or in the glass tower, keep your conspiracy theories or disdain to yourself.

5. Love your car, American or import. You don't have to be an enthusiast, but you shouldn't have to treat your car—essentially, a very expensive robotic pet—as a burden. Maintain it. Get regular oil changes, for goodness sakes—so many people don't! Get that noise checked out, keep your fluids fresh. Keep it clean, too; there will be instances in Detroit where not everybody wants to wait for a cab.

## ADVICE FOR CAR-SPOTTERS

You'd think the Motor City would be a car-spotter's paradise, but...not exactly. A few years ago, a writer for *Jalopnik*, the most-visited car site, joked that all he saw in Detroit during a visit to the North American International Auto Show were Pontiac Azteks. He wasn't exactly correct. You can see some Pontiac Montanas, too.

Detroiters are loyal to the Big Three, no matter how ugly or unremarkable the vehicle, but we're also loyal to cars that will get us through long, snowy winters. We're probably the only city in the world with owners' clubs dedicated to the eighth- and ninth-generation Chevrolet Impala. So that means lots of SUVs and lots of big sedans—even RWD ones, despite their spotty performance in the snow.

But car enthusiasts should fear not, as there are places in and around Detroit where you can get an eyeful. Such as:

## BIRMINGHAM

Among one of the wealthiest suburbs in Southeast Michigan, Birmingham is also one of the showiest. Head to downtown B-ham and see how many Ferraris you can count in half an hour.

## SOUTHWEST DETROIT

You can spot a lowrider or donked Box Chevy anywhere on the east side or west side, especially on the mile roads. But Southwest is hands down the epicenter of car-mod culture in the region. Each year around Cinco de Mayo, residents gather in a church parking lot for the "Blessing of the Lowriders," where a priest prays over the cars and their owners. Donks, SLABS, and lowriders have an unfortunate association with gangs in other cities, but Southwest's culture is borne from true passion for the vehicles as a means of staying *out* of trouble.

## BELLE ISLE

A popular spot for cruisers, Belle Isle offers owners of classic cars a minimal speed limit that lets you slow down and show off. It's also a major spot for owners of heavily modded cars—SLABs and lowriders especially—to let loose.

## YPSILANTI AND ANN ARBOR

Ypsilanti is home to the Ypsilanti Automotive Heritage Museum, a small but worthy honor to some of Detroit's defunct automakers, such as Hudson, Nash, and Tucker. Not only that, but Ypsilanti itself is often the stomping grounds for classic-car owners, with big and small events regularly taking place during warmer months. In neighboring Ann Arbor, one can be run over by the number of Prius models; it is Michigan's most liberal, eco-conscious city after all. But many of the town's quirky residents take pride in maintaining older German and Asian makes. Both cities are college towns with enthusiast students driving a variety of fun models.

### AUBURN HILLS, DEARBORN, MILFORD

Respectively, home to the testing grounds for future Chrysler, Ford, and GM products. Lucky, eagle-eyed spotters—as well as a cottage industry of spy photographers—have seen upcoming models on the road, correctly guessing what's in the pipeline even through heavy camouflage tape.

## CAR-CENTRIC CELEBRATIONS

Yes, we do go all out in celebration of the fine machinery that made this town what it was. Know that there are several events big and small, planned and unplanned. You may be driving down the street and see an impromptu gathering of classic cars. Or modded cars. Or racers. You just never know. Here are some of the bigger events.

### WOODWARD DREAM CRUISE

The biggest celebration of cars in the state, maybe even the whole world. Each year, car enthusiasts follow a route up and down Woodward Avenue with their prized, motorized possessions—the rule is that each car must be at least 25 years old—and show them off, maybe even sell them if they can broker a deal, to fellow car buffs. Be warned that it's also a target for certain groups—anti-abortion activists come to mind—to spread their message to a large crowd.

### AUTORAMA

An indoor custom-car fest that follows the North American International Auto Show; versions of the show are held in other cities, but Detroit being the car capital it is always draws the biggest crowd.

## MOTORCITY GUMBALL RALLY

An intersection of luxury cars and motorsports, the Gumball is a newer annual event with a decidedly younger audience raised on the "Fast and Furious" franchise. Participants and affiliates also hold other events throughout the year.

## CARS & COFFEE EVENTS

Few Cars & Coffee events are held in city limits, but they are regularly held in Detroit suburbs. They are sporadic, so check in with Facebook groups and look for event invites.

## MICHIGAN VINTAGE VOLKSWAGEN FESTIVAL

See, not everyone disdains foreign cars. One of the more unique events on the scene is this annual collection of rare VWs, usually held in Ypsilanti during the spring.

## EAST VS. WEST CAR SHOW

You'll have to keep your ear to the ground for this one. It's never organized, it just seems to pop up organically. It's a donk and SLAB paradise, bringing out fans from, well, the east side and the west side to see which side is the best side. Plenty of footage from past shows is easily found online.

## CRUISIN' GRATIOT

An alternative to the Woodward Dream Cruise, Cruisin' Gratiot is a similar event that makes its way up Gratiot Avenue, a major thoroughfare through the eastside suburbs in Macomb County. (Woodward goes through the western suburbs of Oakland County.) It's usually held in June.

### LINGENFELTER COLLECTION EVENTS

Enthusiasts should know the name Lingenfelter thanks to the company's dedication to performance. But watch Lingenfelter's social media or events pages for ongoing events, including its own Cars & Coffee events, which recently launched.

### SKETCHBATTLE

A newer event that combines street art with car exhibition, Sketchbattle holds two events each year: A car show and "sketch battle" among aspiring car designers in the summer, and a similar battle during auto-show time in January. It's a chance for budding enthusiasts to mix and mingle with industry veterans.

### CONCOURS D'ELEGANCE

An annual vintage car exhibition and auction held each summer in Plymouth, the Concours d'Elegance features a different collection each year. One of the finer classic-car shows in the country.

### EYESON DESIGN CAR SHOW

Held each summer at the Edsel and Eleanor Ford House, this car show is dedicated to design rather than performance. Some of the finest, classic American automobiles are on display.

## THE ONE PLACE ALL GEARHEADS SHOULD VISIT

You can tour the factories here, you can see the performance studios, you can check out the higher-end dealerships to your heart's content, but the one place all automotive aficionados should visit in Detroit is The National Automotive History Collection at the Detroit Public Library's Skillman Branch downtown. It is an archive of the entire automotive industry, from past to present, in one space. From mechanics' manuals and periodicals, to sales figures and product guides, every single scrap of paper having anything to do with cars is here. (And it's all free with a library card.)

## FREEWAY TRAFFIC AND CONSTRUCTION

At any given time during the year, there will be major road construction. And at any time of the year, there will be big events in the region—specifically concerts and sporting events—that gum up traffic. The two of these together can cause nightmares for drivers. Though construction on freeways is sometimes unavoidable, do beware of big events at the downtown sporting and venues and big suburban venues like the Palace of Auburn Hills. Remember, you can always take surface streets; the Mile roads always run east and west.

## THE "WAVE" AND THE MICHIGAN LEFT

There are two quirks about driving here you should be aware of. First, there's the Midwest "wave," which is a brief, polite hand motion to say "thanks" for letting you switch lanes, go forth at a stop sign, or any other way of driving ahead of the driver before you. Does it look like someone is staring dead at you through their windshield? They're waiting for your "wave." The other is the Michigan Left, a local colloquialism for making a complicated left turn. If you're on a road divided by an island and you have to head left onto a street, there's a chance you will not be able to make a left at that intersection. Instead, you will have to go around the island on the next block, head in the other direction and make a right on the street you're trying to get on. That's a Michigan Left.

## ADVICE FOR LEADFOOTS

People like to say Detroit is lawless, but that can't be farther from the truth. For a few years, officers did not patrol as much (not to say they didn't at all) for speeders and other traffic miscreants. Now, police in Detroit are increasingly on the lookout for drivers without seat belts, expired registrations, yellow-light runners (just stop at them if you can), and, of course, speeders. Many main streets in town are unofficially known as "no-tolerance zones," where it basically means you can't talk your way out of the ticket you're about to get. And the last thing you want to do is fight a ticket in 36th District Court, a completely unorganized city court where drivers can spend up to an entire day waiting for a case to be heard alongside every other accused lawbreaker in town.

You may be tempted to go above the limit in and around Detroit on the freeways and major roads. You may get away with it in town (but again, do not treat Detroit as lawless, and don't get pissy if you do get caught), but know that suburban policing is tougher than city policing. County sheriffs and suburban officers regularly nab Detroiters on the border roads like Telegraph Road, Michigan Avenue, and especially Eight Mile Road, where speed limits change between cities or just to remind drivers what side of town they're on. And no one will exactly say this out loud, but the closer to the end of the month, the more intense the policing.

## KNOWN SPEED TRAPS

- On the Lodge crossing into Southfield from Detroit.
- Along eastbound and westbound I-94 in Allen Park and Taylor.
- Anywhere in the vicinity of the airport.
- The entire stretch of M-39 starting at the Dearborn-Detroit border, through Allen Park and where the freeway ends at I-94.
- Telegraph Road in all suburbs.
- I-75 in Troy.
- Square Lake Road in Oakland County and the Square Lake Road exit off southbound I-75.
- Along eastbound and westbound I-96 in Redford.

- Along northbound and southbound I-275 in Farmington Hills and Novi.
- Anywhere on Woodward Avenue through the Oakland County suburbs, especially the underpass between the Pleasant Ridge-Royal Oak border.
- Anywhere on Woodward Avenue in Highland Park. (Yes, Highland Park police will pull you over despite what you've heard about this city.)
- Along the southbound I-75 service drive in Hamtramck.

## WHAT TO DO IF YOU DON'T HAVE A CAR

Fret not, as the explosion of Uber and ZipCar in other markets is also happening here. And if you find yourself in an electric car, we've got charging stations popping up around, too.

*I'm goin' to get me a job up there in*

**MR. FORD'S PLACE.**

*Stop these eatless days from starin' me in the face.*

—Blind Blake, "Detroit Bound Blues"

# CHAPTER 9

## HOW TO DEAL WITH THE MEN IN THIS TOWN

Sometime in the 1990s, it became in vogue for black parents in Detroit to send their children to private school because it looked better on their kids' resume and improved their chances of getting into college. And maybe there were also those parents who just wanted to keep their kids out of trouble by making them wear a uniform every day.

In sixth grade, my mother, brother, and I moved across town from Lafayette Park outside downtown to a house in Russell Woods on the west side. With that came a change of schools, and I transferred from Whitney Young, a public junior high school, to Martyrs of Uganda Academy, a Catholic school near the Motown Historical Museum.

I say the Motown Museum because that's the closest, most recognizable landmark that's still around. The school itself was attached to a church that hadn't been used in at least a decade. The neighborhood, not too far from the epicenter of the 1967 riots, was slowly deteriorating.

M of U, as our gym class T-shirts read, was divided by gender. We had a Catholic religious service once a week, even though many students weren't Catholic. (You could tell who was Catholic by who took communion, though.) There was one priest, who knew about the actual martyrs of Uganda—historical Catholic priests killed in their effort to bring religion to the country. The rest were typical overworked teachers, one of whom carried the same Virginia Slims in her purse my mother used to smoke.

For the sixth-grade boys, our teacher was Mr. Dortch, a tall, would've-been basketball player who wound up in education somehow. The class itself was a mixed bag of personalities. There was Kenneth, a pretty boy with curly hair—but he always smelled like corn chips. There was John, a white boy who loved rap and had no qualms about saying "nigga." There was the big bully Jason, who always came to school with scars or welts on his arms and legs because—as Mr. Dortch told us all one day while he was absent, surely without consent —he was being abused at home. There was Jaylon, a quiet nerd with good handwriting; Mr. Dortch made him write each of our names for honor-roll certificates. And there was Damon, who was smart enough to rank as a nerd, but cool enough to wear CK Be cologne.

I never quite fit in with the boys. I was a crybaby all through elementary school, never in full control of my emotions. I didn't just take things to heart, I took things to a deeper place and couldn't just let go. I'd be teased often because I was such an easy target. That carried over into middle school, unfortunately, but sixth grade toughened me up, for better or for worse.

Mr. Dortch was insistent on teaching us about manhood, and what it means to be a man. Most schools—or hell, most people—teach kids nonviolence. Don't hit back. Tell an adult. Walk away. Not Mr. Dortch. He encouraged fighting; it's what men do. He wanted us to defend ourselves at any cost.

I remember this one discussion, the crux of which was, "Don't be a sissy." Because sissies, as Mr. Dortch taught us, turn into FAGITS —that's how he spelled it on the chalkboard. I had a vague idea of what that was at the time. I knew it meant gay, but I didn't know it was an awful slur. I knew what the term connoted: swishing around, snapping your fingers, and talking funny. Mr. Dortch told us this was wrong.

For whatever reason, I was called sissy and fag a lot. I mean, yeah, people can know that they are gay at a certain age, don't get me wrong. But I was pretty much staying in line with the rest of the boys. I listened to rap music, I played sports. But I was still sensitive. And when I said I was sensitive, Mr. Dortch would mock me with a lisp.

That brand of homophobia was instantly absorbed by my classmates. Once in gym class, I was made fun of for not keeping up in a basketball game. A boy named Persia wanted to fight me because of it. He hit me, I hit him back. I tried to kick him in the nuts, and he pushed me down on the ground when I missed. Then he said I wasn't even worth fighting in the first place because, "You're not a boy, you're just a little girl." I was silent and humiliated for the rest of the day.

How extraordinary was it that a school that preached Christian love had such a hostile environment? By the end of the school year my mother had already enrolled me in a new school for seventh grade. I won't forget the last day at M of U, because while all the boys and girls were outside talking about their plans for the summer, I was in my mom's car almost as soon as the final bell rang. I didn't talk to anyone, didn't say goodbye, didn't get anyone's phone number for a sleepover or playdate. I left Uganda and never looked back.

---

A term new transplants often use for Detroiters is "gritty." They are infatuated with this image of stoic men with grimy hands, prideful and humble all at once, and always in survival mode. There's a very specific kind of man they're talking about here, ranking in the annals next to plaid-wearing farmers, weary truckers, and rope-slinging cowboys. Never in full view of someone's day-to-day existence, but you know they exist somewhere. It's almost folklore.

"Gritty" is such a catch-all term without nuance. I tend to think the men in this town are all like Mr. Dortch: hard-driving bastards with little patience for bullshit.

Men in this town, especially black men, are revered and feared all at once. Many black people believe strongly in Christianity. And the Bible teaches that men lead. The man is the head of the household, the man is served first, the man is the provider, and so on, and so forth. We in Detroit have put consistent faith in men over the years.

Men in Detroit are of a slightly different ilk, though. So many of us are direct descendants of the slave trade, and we know the Southern horror stories passed down from generation to generation. Because our ancestors have never been given what was rightfully owed, we must fight to keep whatever we get. The task has been left up to men to protect those assets.

Men, like the ones in my family, migrated from the South to Detroit with their wives and children, or they sought work and sent for them later. Racism was alive and well in the North, but the North was free from Jim Crow laws and mass lynchings. You could either be a sharecropper in the South and earn little profit from greedy farmers, or you could work for $5 a day in a factory up North. The choice seemed easy.

And so, men led. Women stayed at home and raised the kids while the men worked in the factories. And not just building cars—there was other heavy industry here, too.

Black men in Detroit were not only at charge at home, but also behind some of the social and political movements in Detroit. The Nation of Islam has roots in Detroit, beginning in the 1930s and eventually growing into the organization that graduated Malcolm X—who spent some early years in Detroit—to national prominence. Black labor movements were organized by black men. Black religious movements were organized by black male pastors. All would intertwine in and out over the years, particularly labor and religion.

We have counted on men to lead, so you'll have to understand why undying loyalties—sometimes clouded by bad judgment—to black men in power are often unchallenged.

---

People always ask why people in Detroit elected Mayor Kwame Kilpatrick to a second term when his undoing began in his first. And people always ask why he still has supporters even though he's in prison.

Kilpatrick's backstory starts with the political movement born in the black church. His mother, Carolyn Cheeks Kilpatrick, a former congresswoman, and father, Bernard Kilpatrick, both were active in the Shrine of the Black Madonna, a powerful black church that wielded just as much political clout as it did religious.

With his mother fully entrenched in local and state politics by the time he was old enough to run, it seemed easy enough for the younger Kilpatrick to sail into any political seat of his choice. But he still had to prove himself. Folks in Detroit love a black man, but they love an eloquent, accomplished black man even more. Kilpatrick was both by the time he was ready for mayor.

If you were to take the temperature of Detroit today, folks don't love Kilpatrick as much after the scandal. But there is still a small segment of the population that does. Why? Because despite the scandals, the corruption, the affairs, the rumors, and the prison sentences, folks just love a black male who has done good.

*Kwame Kilpatrick*
*Mayor of Detroit, 2002-2008*

Kilpatrick was once hailed as not just the future of Detroit, but the future of black politics in America. He spoke alongside a young Barack Obama at the Democratic National Convention. He was, as the old folks way, on his way. He was gonna make it! And then he fucked up.

Admitting that Kilpatrick fucked up has been hard for many, because we are often suspicious of what really happens when a black man in power is taken down. Certainly there have been instances where black men were conspired against when they climbed too far up the ladder. Kilpatrick doesn't fit that mold; he was his own undoing. But there are people that feel that way, and you'll just have to forgive them.

Try not to argue or wag your finger if you run into a Kilpatrick defender. Because to them, they are not just defending Kilpatrick—they're defending the dignity of the black male in Detroit. The black men who fought so hard for us to live the middle-class lifestyles promised to us when we arrived here from the South. The black men who kept the bills paid in the house and kept the kids in line and out of trouble. It is natural for us to always want to find the good in our black men, even those who fuck up just as bad as Kwame.

---

When I was 16 and confused about life, my grandfather once told me there's no better place for a black man to be than in America.

Wayne State University in Detroit's Midtown area is hailed as a paragon of diversity, but it hasn't always been so. In the 1960s, my grandfather attempted to obtain a master's degree in nursing from WSU. Professors asked why a man, a black man, wanted to become a nurse. They didn't think he'd be able to complete the program; he eventually did, and became the school's first black male graduate to finish it.

There's no better place for black men in America because despite it all, where else would we have this kind of opportunity? We had this conversation in the kitchen of his home in Indian Village. Looking around, it was hard to disagree.

But that was more than a decade ago. It now feels like open season on black men—and women, let's not get this wrong—with us being murdered at every turn. It's beginning to get more and more comfortable to ask whether America is really here for us. Is it?

In Detroit, black men are not an endangered species, hunted for sport. There are incidents where we have been on the wrong end of a police officer's baton or gun. But I wonder if we are safer here than, say, down South where so many of us have ancestral homes.

The black man in Detroit is complicated. He is not perfect, he is flawed. He means well, and sometimes he can be a hardass. But he is loved here, regardless. He will make a way, make the best of his means, and he will have opportunity here. This is exactly why we are here to begin with.

*Only when we are honest about our issues*

**CAN WE TRULY SOLVE THEM.**

—Kym Worthy, Wayne County Prosecutor

# CHAPTER 10

## HOW TO BE A WOMAN IN THIS TOWN

Actually, no. Ignore that chapter title, because I sure as sugar can't tell you how to be a woman in Detroit. Because, well, I just don't have any experience in that area. Zero. None.

I don't want to mansplain, I don't want to put my arm around you and give you the "hey, ladies" tour of Detroit. I'll say right away—if you're wondering—that we have no shortage of clinics and other facilities that address women's health. But let's be clear that I'm not saying that a woman should only care about her health. I am just guessing that if you're moving here and unfamiliar with Detroit, you will want to know right away that your body will be taken care of.

I could speak to how women are treated socially in Detroit. And again, if we're being honest—it's not always that great. Of course this is true for women everywhere. But because Detroit—America—has been so male-dominated, women's accomplishments have not always been greeted here with the accolades their male counterparts garner.

But do we love women in Detroit? Yes. Very much so. We could do better in treating women with respect. I'm not talking about catcalling on the street (it may happen) or breaking the glass ceiling (even though a woman is in charge of General Motors, not every workplace is in the same league). I'm saying that respecting women means not treating them like a footnote in the history of this town, and making sure they're not an afterthought in the city's future.

---

Before you arrived in Detroit, you may have heard of a woman named Monica Conyers. She is the wife of John Conyers, who, as of this book's publication, is currently the longest-serving member of Congress.

John Conyers was born in 1929 and was first elected to represent Detroit (and surrounding areas) in the House of Representatives in 1965. Monica Conyers wasn't even a year old when he was first elected.

Younger woman, older man. Isn't that the way it always goes? Monica married John when she was 25. He was 61, and, of course, still in Congress. (He's probably going to die with his boots on, by the way.) She took Conyers' surname, and when your last name is Conyers in Detroit, you can go almost anywhere. Monica Conyers went to City Council.

It's kind of an open secret that in Detroit, voters often vote based on name recognition. Now granted, you probably can't poll everyone who voted in City Council elections in the last few decades and ask if they voted for Monica Conyers based on her name alone. But considering she had no political experience before being voted to the Council in 2005, you have to wonder.

Here's where you may have heard about Conyers. A few years ago, Conyers and former City Council President Ken Cockrel Jr. (Ken Cockrel Sr. was a councilman as well, but the junior's credentials before political life are legit, so the "name recognition" argument may not apply here) got into a heated argument at an open council meeting, and Conyers repeatedly called Cockrel "Shrek." So former *Detroit News* reporter Charlie LeDuff set up a meeting with Conyers and some middle-school students to discuss her conduct, and filmed it for the newspaper's website.

One of the students asked Conyers why she, an adult politician, was calling another adult schoolyard names. "We're human, but we have to know our boundaries," the student told Conyers. And the two went back and forth—an adult debating someone not old enough for a learner's permit, let's remember this—until it ended with the student having the last word. Detroiters were shocked that a city councilwoman got wicked burned by a teenybopper. The rest of the world laughed as the video spread, another example of this city's incompetence.

Before the "Shrek" fallout, Conyers' qualifications to serve on council were dubious. Afterward, there was no doubt. She was later charged with corruption, and did some time in a minimum-security federal prison.

For every Monica Conyers, there are many more women in Detroit who strive to prove themselves in a climate where women are seen as accessories, hangers-on, or beneficiaries of nepotism of men. And now that the world knows that a grown woman can be so easily schooled by an eighth grader, we dilute the legacy by great women that have made an impact in Detroit.

---

Could anyone love you like a black woman? There is no comparable affection, in my opinion: Unconditional, unrestrained, a type of love that's tender and tough at once, and impossible to forget. Those of us blessed with the good fortune to have been loved by a black woman are forever in their debt.

I am in deep thought about the love of black women as I read on and on about the welcoming women of the Wednesday night Bible study at Emanuel African Methodist Episcopal Church in Charleston, S.C., where no additional words are needed to describe the horrendous crime that unfolded there. But also, I am thinking of black women here in Detroit—specifically, the teachers in our public schools.

There is a retired teacher, Carole Watson, who came to Detroit from Mississippi years ago and taught in several public schools. Today, she is spearheading a movement known as Us Too, Detroit, an effort to promote the black businesses that kept the lights on in Detroit before the new wave of residents moved in. When I met her, she gave me the warmest hug that felt all too familiar.

Black female teachers in Detroit are special, and they are unsung. Watson reminded me of several teachers I had in DPS in almost all grades: Lots of jewelry, a warm fragrance, a big smile, overflowing with knowledge. I had a lot of those grandmotherly, auntie-types back in the day.

Many of Detroit's schools now are stocked with fresh, young graduates by way of AmeriCorps or Teach For America. Now let's be clear that I'm not saying that younger teachers don't or won't have the same impact as those old-school teachers I'm used to. I'm just saying that a city that was mostly black for a long time with a mostly black school system had a certain kind of love that you probably can't find elsewhere.

Those are the women that we love here, and those are the women whose accomplishments should not go unnoticed. And there are more, and they're not all black. I think of Grace Lee Boggs, the Chinese-American activist who relocated here in the 1950s and has become an icon of social justice. I think of Eleanor Josaitis, a white woman from Taylor who co-founded Focus: HOPE with two Catholic priests to serve the poor in the wake of the 1967 riots. I think of Viola Liuzzo, the Teamsters wife and Wayne State student killed by the KKK for daring to stand with the NAACP during the civil rights movement. I think of Maryann Mahaffey, a white woman who won over black voters to be elected to city council long before our current mayor took office.

We are seeing now emerging women leaders from the city's Latino and Arab-American communities. And we are seeing women from outside Detroit make inroads in entrepreneurship. I am confident, though, that in this town—this mostly black town—that there is a certain magic that comes with being a black woman.

---

The infant mortality rate in Detroit, according to a recent report in the Detroit News, is the worst among large cities in the U.S. Women in Detroit are not getting the resources they need to deliver a healthy baby to term.

Only recently have thousands of rape kits, left untested in an abandoned Detroit police facility for years, been processed. Still, I will wager that many women who have been victims of rape over the last few decades will never see their rapists tried.

We may individually love our women, but women still are being failed here at every turn. Some boys aren't taught not to hit. Some teachers don't know how to deal with teen girls filled with angst. Some relatives don't know sexual boundaries. But our infrastructure and social systems, at the very least, should know better.

I can't offer advice on being a woman new to Detroit, except for this: empathize with your fellow female citizens. Understand that as a newbie, you may have certain advantages that the next woman doesn't. But also understand that we—not just us men, but all of us as Detroiters—are trying. I can't say when things will get better for women here. But like with many things Detroit, we can hope that they will.

**DETROIT REPRESENTS ME.**
*I wrote songs because I'm from this city.*

—El DeBarge

# CHAPTER 11

## HOW TO PARTY LIKE A DETROITER

There has been plenty written about Detroit rock bands and Motown. There have been more than enough movies about Detroit, some obviously better than others. And Lord knows there are plenty of books about Detroit. I just want to talk for a brief second about styles and music that we don't always talk about.

There is just something uniquely Detroit about the way we dress and listen to music here. Everyone dresses to the nines, even during hard times. The city is overflowing with musical talent, meaning we'll always have a wealth of tunes in our cultural jukebox. And if we have nothing else to show for ourselves, you'd better be quick on your feet. This is the Detroit I know. This is the Detroit I love.

## FASHIONS UNIQUE TO DETROIT

### GATORS

Someone has yet to delve into the comprehensive history of why gators—dress shoes made from alligator skin and dyed nearly every color of the rainbow—became popular in Detroit. Rumor has it it's because pimps wore them, and people just aspired to be like pimps.

They later became popular among preachers—and there are no rules saying pimps can't be preachers. Regardless, the famous shoe style shouted out by the Notorious B.I.G. in "Hypnotize" ("Stink pink gators, my Detroit playas") holds a special place in the hearts of Detroiters. They're mostly reserved for the older set now, but a stylish young lady or gent can still pull them off.

## CARTIER GLASSES

So we love our designer names in Detroit, and one of the most popular status symbols since the '90s are Cartier glasses. Some call them "yays," after the last syllable of the French surname. Other call them "buffs." They are popular among local rappers, dope boys, and club promoters—three groups of people that are often shot or robbed for wearing these expensive shades, characterized by their wooden arms and metal frames. That's no shade. It's one of those sad-but-true things that comes up on the local news far too often.

## FUR

One of Detroit's earliest industries was fur-trapping, a practice that still exists to this day—though you don't see foxes and minks running around the place like back in the 1700s. Because furriers have been in Detroit since the beginning, fur coats and other fur pieces are had by everyone across social classes, whether they can buy one off the rack with pocket change or have to save up for a time to acquire one. For a while, department stores like Macy's had fur storage and fur salons, though that practice is dying out as department stores shutter. Stores that specialize in fur, such as Detroit's legendary Dittrich Furs (they have a jingle that's familiar to longtime residents), have weathered the toughest times, though.

## QUILTED LEATHER JACKETS

Popularized by local designer Marc Buchanan's Pelle Pelle brand, the Al Wissam boutique in Dearborn, and other style savants, these leather jackets with intricate stitching have outlasted other winter trends (remember those awful NASCAR-style jackets from the 2000s?) to become a Detroit original.

### FEDORAS, APPLEJACKS, AND BOWLERS

We love our elaborate hats here in the city; you did see what Aretha Franklin wore when she sang at President Barack Obama's first inauguration, right? But for something less elaborate, folks here love to top off a fine suit, a short set, anything with buttons with some stylish headwear.

### OLDE ENGLISH "D" HATS

You don't even have to be a Tigers fan to rock the "D" hat. Which means if you do see someone wearing one, don't expect them to rattle off a bunch of stats from the last game.

## QUIET STORM: THE SOUNDTRACK FOR SEXY TIMES IN THE CITY

Quiet storm is what we call a certain kind of R&B music played in the nighttime hours. It's a popular genre among radio DJs and named after the Smokey Robinson song of the same name. In laymen's terms, it's "slower" R&B. Here in Detroit, there's an added layer, because we have produced so many musicians that may or may not have made it to the upper stratosphere of pop music, but they all made songs that forever claim a place on the mixtapes of locals.

"I Just Wanna Be Your Girl" **CHAPTER 8***

"Key to The World" **L.J. REYNOLDS**

"My Favorite Thing" **CALVIN BROOKS FEATURING HARI PARIS**

"Something in the Past" **ONE WAY**

"If You Play Your Cards Right" **ALICIA MYERS**

"Soulful Moaning" **DALE**

"Just Roll" **FABU**

"Can't We Fall in Love Again" **MICHAEL HENDERSON AND PHYLLIS HYMAN****

"You Are My Starship" **NORMAN CONNORS FEATURING MICHAEL HENDERSON**

"Can't Get Enough" **WILLIE MAX FEATURING RAPHAEL SADDIQ****

"So Good" **DAVINA**

"It's You That I Need" **ENCHANTMENT**

"Gloria" **ENCHANTMENT**

"Kissing You" **KEITH WASHINGTON**

"Candlelight and You" **KEITH WASHINGTON AND CHANTE MOORE****

"On the Ocean" **K'JON**

"Nights Over Egypt" **THE JONES GIRLS**

"Who Can I Run To?" **THE JONES GIRLS**

"Saturday Love" **CHERELLE AND ALEXANDER O'NEAL****

"Everything I Miss At Home" **CHERELLE**

"Footsteps in the Dark" **BODY**

"Ev'ry Little Bit" **MILLIE SCOTT**

"Tell 'Em What They Wanna Hear" **RASHAD MORGAN**

"I'mma Love You Right" **JOHN BROWN**

"Heaven in Your Arms" **R.J.'S LATEST ARRIVAL**

"I Get High (Off Your Memory)" **FREDA PAYNE**

"Trouble" **BEI MAEJOR FEATURING T.I.****

"Do Your Thing" **7 MILE**

"No Place to Go" **PERRI**

"Almost Wrote You A Love Song" **BIG SEAN FEATURING SUAI**

"Ambiguous" **BIG SEAN, MIKE POSNER AND CLINTON SPARKS****

**Chapter 8 was fronted by Anita Baker until she went solo and became a superstar. Baker is the indisputable queen of Detroit quiet storm and has an expansive catalogue, but we're focusing on the lesser-known cuts.*

***Neither Hyman, Saddiq, Moore, O'Neal, T.I., or Sparks are from Detroit, a disclaimer that has to be added for the purists reading this.*

## MOTOWN TRIVIA FOR YOUR NEXT PARTY

Aretha Franklin was the Queen of Soul, but she was not the Queen of Motown. There are a surprising number of people who assume that every artist from Detroit recorded for Motown, when in truth Detroit was home to quite a few indie labels during its heyday. And that's not even counting folks like Franklin, who began her professional recording career far away from Detroit. Similarly, every Motown artist was not from Detroit; the label was indeed an incubator for homegrown stars, but it also recruited from across the country.

*Aretha Franklin*

## FROM DETROIT AND DIDN'T RECORD FOR MOTOWN

### ARETHA FRANKLIN

Though her star rose at the same time that Motown Records became a force, Franklin never recorded for the label. Her string of hits was issued on Columbia, Atlantic, and Arista—but her first-ever recording was at a small record shop in Paradise Valley.

### ANITA BAKER

Alongside Whitney Houston and Janet Jackson, she ruled 1980s R&B with a special blend of jazz and soul perfected by Detroit producer Michael Powell. But her career prime came as Motown's lights began to flicker.

## THE DRAMATICS

Motown already had the Temptations and the Four Tops, but this group with roots in Pershing High School on the east side rivaled them with cuts like "Whatcha See is Whatcha Get," "In The Rain," "Just Shopping," "Be My Girl," and "Door to Your Heart."

## RAY PARKER, JR.

The *Ghostbusters* theme is how you know him. Detroiters recognize cuts like "A Woman Needs Love" and "For Those Who Like to Groove" —both with his band Raydio. He also wrote for other artists, helping solidify New Edition's place in boy-band history with "Mr. Telephone Man." But despite attending high school at Northwestern, a few blocks down from Motown Studios, he never recorded for the label.

## AALIYAH

She was born in Brooklyn, but raised here in Detroit, so we claim her. Go to the Detroit School of Arts, her alma mater, and you'll see a large portrait of her in the hallway. There's debate outside Detroit on how big Aaliyah's influence is on 1990s and 2000s R&B, but here in the city, she's an undeniable princess. Try and go a day without hearing "Rock the Boat" on urban radio.

## THE CLARK SISTERS AND THE WINANS

Motown dabbled in gospel, but neither of the first families of Detroit gospel crossed paths with the label. The Clark Sisters, all of whom still live in the area, are best known for "You Brought the Sunshine," a reggae-flavored inspirational tune that found its way to Studio 54 in the early 1980s. You'll hear more about business dealings from the Winans (some legal, some not) more than their music these days, but the original Winans family was influential in contemporary gospel while younger generations—particularly BeBe and CeCe Winans, who ushered in an urban-crossover style of gospel in the 1990s—continue to make music.

### MOST OF THE ROCK STARS

Motown had one big rock act, the Detroit-bred Rare Earth in the 1970s. Everyone else—Bob Seger, Alice Cooper, Ted Nugent, MC5, The White Stripes, Insane Clown Posse, Death, Kid Rock—was not Motown-affiliated.

### NONE OF THE RAPPERS

You'd be hard-pressed to name any rap album released on Motown. None of Detroit's current crop of rappers—Big Sean, Eminem and the rest of D12, Dej Loaf, Trick Trick, Black Milk, Slum Village, Danny Brown, Royce da 5'9—ever recorded for the label.

## FROM DETROIT, RECORDED FOR MOTOWN, BUT ALSO FOUND SUCCESS OUTSIDE OF MOTOWN

### THE SPINNERS

They first landed a Motown hit with the Stevie Wonder-penned "It's A Shame" in 1970. They found greater success with Philly soul producer Thom Bell and a string of hits including "Could It Be I'm Falling in Love," "Rubberband Man," and the can't-escape-on-Mother's-Day "Sadie."

### EL DEBARGE

The Detroit-born, Grand Rapids-raised singer with the unmistakable falsetto scored big Motown hits with his siblings, including "Rhythm of the Night" and the still-played-on-urban-radio slow jams "All This Love," "I Like It," "Love Me In A Special Way," and "A Dream." When he staged a comeback in 2010 and won his way back into Detroit hustlers' hearts with "Lay With You" on the *Second Chance* album, it wasn't with Motown.

### ASHFORD AND SIMPSON

Though technically Valerie Simpson is from New York, her success came when pairing up with Ypsilanti-raised songwriter Nick Ashford at Motown. They wrote some of your Motown favorites for other artists, like "Ain't No Mountain High Enough" and "You're All I Need to Get By." Their recognizable success comes from recording as a duo after leaving Motown, giving us "Solid" and "It Seems To Hang On." They also wrote "I'm Every Woman" for Chaka Khan and "The Boss" for Diana Ross.

## NOT FROM DETROIT AND RECORDED FOR MOTOWN

### GLADYS KNIGHT AND THE PIPS

Most don't know that this group's origins began in Atlanta. After recording regional hits there, the group signed with Berry Gordy and gave us Motown cuts like "I Heard it Through the Grapevine" and "If I Were Your Woman." Arguably, their greatest success came after leaving Motown, where they cut the big hits like "Midnight Train to Georgia" and their cover of "The Way We Were."

### MARVIN GAYE

Gaye was deeply entrenched in Detroit (and Motown, since he married Berry Gordy's sister), making a home on Appoline Street on the city's west side and, at one point, trying out for the Detroit Lions. But the "What's Going On" singer was from Washington, D.C. (Incidentally, frequent duet partner Tammi Terrell also was not a Detroit native; she was from Philadelphia.)

### THE COMMODORES AND LIONEL RICHIE

The Commodores and their eventual solo star Lionel Richie have origins at Tuskegee University in Alabama. Their song "Zoom" was never released as a single, but it is a quiet storm classic on Detroit radio. The Richie-led hymn "Jesus is Love" is a favorite in the local churches.

## THE ISLEY BROTHERS

Though briefly affiliated with Motown in the 1960s, their earliest hit, "Shout," did not come by way of the label, and neither did their stellar run in the 1970s and 1980s with songs like "Fight the Power," "For the Love Of You," "Who's That Lady," and "Between the Sheets." Their biggest Motown hit, however, was "This Old Heart of Mine."

## TEENA MARIE

Called the Ivory Queen of Soul, and certainly not be confused with the Queen of Soul, the white singer with the black voice was from California, but had nothing but love for Detroit while she lived. Her producer, **RICK JAMES**, wasn't a Detroiter either, but James' uncle, Melvin Franklin, was one of the Temptations. The pair's duet, "Fire and Desire," is still popular on Detroit radio, and was featured in a memorable scene from the Detroit-based sitcom "Martin."

## THE JACKSON 5 AND MICHAEL JACKSON

I mean, you should already know they're from Gary, Indiana. But the Jacksons kicked their career into high gear in Detroit, although not for that long. Their success came just as the company uprooted and moved to California. Their success was also the beginning of the end of Motown's dominance as a record label; Berry Gordy once referred to them as "the last big stars to come rolling off my assembly line."

# WATCH MY FEET: HOW TO DANCE LIKE A DETROITER

We love to dance in Detroit. Every region has its own style, like shagging in the Carolinas or krumping in Southern California. Many of the styles that emerged from this city are tied to working in tandem with other dancers. These include hustles, ballrooming, and jitting.

## HUSTLE

A Detroit "hustle" is a line dance – do not call it the electric slide – that ranges from simple shuffling and half-turns to more intricate footwork, arm movements, and multiple turns. Hustles are often performed at weddings, picnics, and other social events. In other regions, like Chicago, the dance can be called "stepping," but here, we call it hustling. Four-on-the-floor beats are best for these performances.

## BALLROOMING

A close cousin of hustle, usually performed in pairs. Like Detroit hustles, the footwork is complex, yet both parties must remain in step, as the dance is also intimate. Generally one person leads, though the move is so smooth, you can't even tell half the time.

## JIT

A Detroit street dance with roots in gang battles in the '70s that's far more high-energy than hustles or ballrooming. It began with a group called the Jitterbugs, who were featured in the recent film The Jitterbugs: Pioneers of the Jit. Again, footwork is key – though jitting is rapid-fire tapping, crossing, and shuffling coupled with rapid torso and arm movements, even kicks and flips. It's not quite breakdancing, as it never reaches the level of head-spinning and such. What separates jit from other regional styles is that it's tied directly to a form of Detroit electronic music called ghettotech: gritty, unpolished techno that sometimes has raunchy lyrics.

## SOME POPULAR DETROIT HUSTLE AND BALLROOM SONGS

"My Eyes Don't Cry," **STEVIE WONDER**

"Feels So Right," **JANET JACKSON**

"All I Do," **KIRK WHALUM FEATURING WENDY MOTEN**

"I Want," **CHAKA KHAN**

"Bartender," **T-PAIN AND AKON**

"Slow Down," **BOBBY VALENTINO**

"Before I Let Go," **MAZE FEATURING FRANKIE BEVERLY**

"Just in Case," **JAHEIM**

"The Floor," **JOHNNY GILL**

# SOME—AND I DO MEAN *SOME*—POPULAR DETROIT JIT SONGS

"Timeline" **GALAXY 2 GALAXY***

"Percolator" **CAJMERE**

"Godzilla Mix" **DJ SNOWFLAKE**

"Uh-Oh, Work It, Work It" **DJ SNOWFLAKE**

"Let Me Bang" **DJ DEEON**

"Sex on the Beach" **MR. DE AND GREG C. BROWN**

"Gel-N-Weave" **DJ ASSAULT**

* *A sped-up version of the original is the "jit" version.*

*School's out for summer. School's out for forever.*

**SCHOOL'S BEEN BLOWN TO PIECES.**

—Alice Cooper, "School's Out"

# CHAPTER 12

## HOW TO RAISE A DETROIT KID

It is difficult to say nice things about the schools in Detroit. Upon moving here, you'll find out that there are two public school districts, a slew of charter schools, and a handful of parochial or private schools. It wasn't always this way.

Back in the day—and for Detroit measures, back in the day is only a few years ago—there was only one public school district, Detroit Public Schools. And for a time, DPS was thriving.

I mentioned earlier that many Detroiters identify themselves by what high school they went to. Some even go as far as to note their elementary and middle schools. Each school has an identity beyond its mascot. Many are strongly tied to neighborhoods and the people that inhabit them. Some are known as athletic powerhouses, graduating future pro athletes. And some, particularly the magnet schools, are known for their academic tracks; you'll meet a *lot* of people who went to Bates Academy, a top-tier elementary and middle school, and you'll meet a *lot* of people who went to Cass, King, or Renaissance, which once reigned as the top three magnet high schools citywide.

Back then, when work was plentiful, even the worst DPS schools could send its graduates to a steady post-secondary job. Obviously, with the economic collapse, jobs are no longer as plentiful. Financial turmoil led white residents to leave Detroit for the suburbs, and after white flight, many blacks followed. A consistent, but not-as-discussed, statistic is that Detroit loses more residents between ages 0-18 than any other demographic. Those are parents taking their kids to other school districts in other cities, because as the population declined, so did the quality of the schools.

A few factors led to DPS' decline. One, other school districts in surrounding suburbs became schools of choice, meaning they could open their doors to students who didn't live in those schools' cities. In Michigan, funding is tied to enrollment, and districts can boost enrollment by siphoning off students from other districts. Next, as population declined in the city, so did enrollment in the city's schools. One by one, Detroit began closing schools and consolidating students in those that remained. Neighborhoods that once thrived now struggle with empty, scrapped schools. Classroom sizes doubled in some of the schools that remained, further decreasing the quality of education—and offering another reason for parents to look, or move, elsewhere.

I'm not even going to pretend to be a psychologist, but I know that when schools are failing and teachers are stressed and things in the neighborhoods are going awry, students are not going to perform at their highest level. I saw firsthand how far Detroit schools had fallen when I was an education reporter covering the district in 2011 and 2012.

Detroit Public Schools had gone into state receivership, which meant it was no longer overseen by the city-elected board but by the state of Michigan. When a public school district in Michigan goes into receivership, the state can appoint—without citizen input, mind you—an emergency manager to steer the ship. As I write, DPS is on its fourth emergency manager in a decade. Some were better than others; the first, Robert Bobb, cleaned house by challenging fraudulent contracts and curbing paychecks sent to fake employees. But there's still the challenge of attracting students to the district as well as preserving quality of education for those already there. With the EM door revolving, there still have been few surface-level results, as test scores remain dismal, enrollment keeps falling, and several schools have closed.

In 2012, Michigan Gov. Rick Snyder announced his intent to spin off some Detroit schools into a second district. The second district would be called Education Achievement Authority, overseen by a state-appointed board and operating on a near-full calendar year, instead of a typical academic year with a nice, long summer vacation.

The schools that would enter into the EAA would be the worst of the worst DPS schools, and the EAA was mandated to turn these schools around under the new regime.

There was one problem, and that was that one DPS high school, Kettering, would close and its student body would be absorbed by Southeastern, a DPS school that was targeted by EAA. Parents at both schools worried that rival gangs would clash once the student bodies were combined. (Ever seen *Degrassi: The New Generation* when the one high school across town burned down and all those kids had to transfer to Degrassi High, and there was like, totally drama because of it? Yeah, this wasn't *Degrassi.*)

After it was formally announced that Kettering would close, I went over to Southeastern to talk to students and teachers about their fears, if any. I visited Southeastern after the final bell rang, hoping to catch a few staff before they went home for the day and maybe a few students. It didn't go as planned.

I walk in the door, and there's a huge fight between two female students by the back entrance. Hair pulling, punches and kicks, the whole nine. Seems like it would be simple to break up two teenage girls, right? Apparently not. A swarm of big, male security guards, some of them carrying guns, came into the fracas. Each girl was wrestled down to the concrete by a respective guard, while other guards pepper-sprayed—pepper spray!—students to get away. The two girls were taken into custody while other bystanders complained about burning eyes and breathing troubles.

Not too long after that fight, another girl fight broke out. This time, I pulled out my phone as security guards and Detroit Public Schools officers—DPS has its own police force, by the way, and they are allowed to carry guns—forcefully broke them apart. Except I was breaking a rule myself. I didn't know it was against school policy to film a fight on school grounds, and suddenly a guard was charging toward me, snatching my phone away and putting me in handcuffs.

I was held in a security room, a room with a cell and a bunch of monitors I had no idea schools even had. After I had explained that I was a reporter, the guards made me delete the fight video and confiscated my phone, telling me to pick it up at the DPS police precinct the next day.

When you grow up in Detroit, you hear about certain schools with certain reputations, but it had never been this bad.

---

Not all Detroit schools are bad, but the good ones are increasingly harder to find. So, too, are the things for kids to do outside of school. I'm not a parent, but I don't envy those that are.

If you live in New York, you may have seen a billboard encouraging you to move to Detroit. Or you don't live in New York but you've seen a snarky New York-based blog's hot take on a billboard encouraging New Yorkers to move to Detroit. As a Detroiter, I can say that yes, Detroit is welcome to anyone. Just leave your kids in Brooklyn, please.

Yes, Detroit will take your tired, your poor, and all the huddled masses yearning to breathe free, but not any of those crumb-snatching blobs of cellular matter you refer to as "children." You see, in order for us to move forward as a city, we simply cannot have children as part of the restorative populace.

A new restaurant opens every week in what was once the nation's fattest city. It is required that beef tartare and some type of cooked cephalopod appear on each menu, and while both front- and back-of-house staffers are a diverse mix of blacks and whites and perhaps an occasional Latino, at least one bartender must have a tattoo sleeve. There are no kids' menus.

Knowing that restaurants are the future, the city administration will allow developers to remake a historic recreation center into a restaurant. There will be housing, even low-income housing for you starving artists. But there will also be another restaurant, just two blocks away from a housing project where a woman's ex-boyfriend shot her 8-year-old son while he slept.

There will also be a beer garden on top of the old recreation center, so no kids allowed there either, because they're not old enough. And sure, it's incongruous that you can get drunk and get fat in the place where the Brown Bomber himself kept fit, but that's where we seem to be headed in New Detroit. Whitney Houston once believed that children are the future. Despite filling her last-ever prescription here, she clearly was not talking about Detroit. Beer, be it in garden or microbrewery form, is the future. And who needs another recreation center, right?

It's all laid out here for the aspiring Detroiter. We already have your yoga studios and dog parks, but we're just not sure what to do with your children. Public transportation is such that you wouldn't want your kids riding alone on them. But hell, most adults don't want to ride the buses here anyway. Go get yourself a bicycle from Shinola, then. (They don't have kids' bikes, for the record.)

Sure, an optimistic parent could wait for pie pushers and barbecue barons to save Detroit by ever-so-slowly rebuilding the tax base —one small plate at a time!—so that public schools could be properly funded. Maybe the infant mortality rate will drop by that time, too. But in the meantime, Detroit really is a DINK paradise.

If you do get pregnant, you could embark on the decathlon-like challenge of enrolling your child in one of the good schools, a process that involves going to open houses announced online in an barely connected city, calling around to schools months ahead of time to ensure enrollment, or maybe be placed in a lottery system where you'll compete with desperate parents from all across the city avoiding the pitfalls of a neighborhood school controlled by one of two underfunded state-run districts.

Are you still absolutely insistent on bringing your children to a city where there are more vacant schools than functioning ones? You may have to live in a suburb. Looking for diversity with that Bushwick edge? Try Hamtramck. Looking for diversity and don't want your car broken into? Try Berkley. Or if you want the prestige of a Manhattan private school, go to Bloomfield Hills, a suburb that most recently made the news when a young black child filmed video of white children taunting him with racial slurs.

It's going to be a tough go of it when you bring your kids here. There are things for kids to do like the Michigan Science Center, the Detroit Institute of Arts, the beach on Belle Isle (or that fake beach at Campus Martius), and other haunts in and around downtown. But know that if you choose to live in a neighborhood downtown, the nearby park may not always be maintained, there may not be a top-notch recreation center, and the neighborhood school may not be up to par.

## SO HOW DO YOU MAKE A GOOD ENVIRONMENT FOR YOUR CHILDREN?

1. Talk to other parents, and not just the ones who look like you. Talk to them about their experiences with schools, the things

they do with their children after school hours, places to shop, places to eat, everything. The one thing about Detroit is that every parent is always discovering something new for their child to get into, because every parent is looking for an opportunity to keep their children stimulated.

2. Be prepared to do a lot of research on schools and child activities, and get ready for a workout. You might find out about schools via the internet; the websites Excellent Schools Detroit and Detroit Parent Network are both gateways to ideal choices for your child. And you might find out by word-of-mouth; that's where talking to other parents comes in. Either way, you should probably do the footwork to check out every institution in person. Be as well prepared for waiting lists and lotteries, as many parents compete for limited slots in everything, be it a school or a summer camp.

3. Teach your child the basics of diversity. It may help to explain very basic things, like varying skin tones and what they mean, to more intricate distinctions, like explaining that not all Latinos know Spanish or the difference between a *hijab* and a *burqa*.

4. Know that your experience is not the next parent's experience. OK, so you were able to get your kid into the best preschool, and there's a good chance they're on the right track to the best elementary school, and it's all smooth sailing to an Ivy League, right? Well, good for you—but every parent doesn't have the same opportunities. Be it the price of paying for tuition of some of these institutions, the convenience of living near some of the good schools or even things like transportation to some of these places, not everyone can do what you do. Don't pooh-pooh other parents who don't have the same ability to make the choices you have at your disposal.

5. You have day care options, and your child will have fun outside of day care. There are many day-care facilities affiliated with hospitals, churches, and other large organizations. When you're free, places like the Michigan Science Center, the Detroit Institute of Arts, the attractions on Belle Isle, and the Detroit Public Libraries are here to keep your child entertained.

6. Remember, anything can happen. A "good" school can close without proper funding. A charter school can change management. A museum can be at risk of shutting down. You might decide to change neighborhoods, or you may choose to leave the city completely. In the old days of Detroit, it was pretty much a straight shot when it came to schooling your kids and keeping them occupied. These days, it's a precarious situation where, really, anything can happen. Stay on your toes.

*Boy, would you boss up and*

**GET THIS MONEY?**

—Blade Icewood, "Boy Would You"

# CHAPTER 13

## HOW TO DO BUSINESS IN DETROIT

I fucking love Vernors Ginger Ale. I know I said coneys were pretty unremarkable, but there's a strong argument that Vernor's better represents the ingenuity and spirit of Detroit than the hot dogs.

Vernor's is a crisp, slightly sweet ginger ale that was developed by one of those old-timey pharmacists who sold prescriptions and sodas. It is not available on a wide scale nationwide. It is available throughout Michigan, scattered across the Midwest, and in rare occasions elsewhere in the country, but it's one of those regional things the majority of Americans are vaguely familiar with, but don't have a complete idea.

Detroit has Faygo pop and had Stroh's beer, but Vernors is incomparable. My mother will kill me for giving away the family recipe, but whenever my grandmother had a social gathering at her home, she made her special punch—Vernors and frozen strawberries in a crystal punch bowl. I was worried that when I left southeast Michigan, where you can find Vernors in every party store and gas station, for mid-Michigan for college, I wouldn't find my favorite pop. The first night I slept in my dorm, I found that the Subway just across the street had Vernors in its fountain machine. I went there every night for a time.

Vernors is legendary among Detroiters not only for its taste, but as a cure for upset stomachs. Or indigestion. Whatever trouble you might be having around there, Vernors—some might take it warm, others cold—can help. Anytime I've eaten something that just won't go down all the way? Vernors is Liquid Plumr. If I need to belch? Vernors gets it out. Neither Canada Dry nor Faygo's Gold flavor does the trick. Try Vernors! You won't be disappointed.

Because Vernors is so beloved among Detroiters—a street is named for its creator—it is authentically Detroit. The company started in 1866, and although it it's no longer made in Detroit—it's now a brand of RC Cola and is bottled in Texas—it's one of those undeniably Detroit things that is symbolic with the city. It's on the short list of companies, brands or products that are truly Detroit; I'd also include Faygo, Better Made, the house-made remedies at Davis Cut-Rate Drugs, the car companies, Carhartt, Dittrich Furs, Little Caesars, and Sanders.

And then you have Shinola.

You've probably heard of Shinola. In fact, the buzz around Shinola might be one of the reasons you've decided to move here. But if you've been living under a rock, here's the rundown: Shinola is a watch manufacturer based in Detroit. In Midtown, to be exact.

Shinola was founded in 2011 after the brains behind the operation purchased the intellectual property of a shoeshine company. Remember *The Jerk* with Steve Martin? Remember that "shit or Shinola" line? That would be the same Shinola brand. Except this time around, the company would make luxury goods in addition to shoe polish, with a focus on leather, bicycles, and their flagship watches.

To make all this stuff, Shinola hired a ton of people from Detroit. That would have been well enough, but Shinola then launched an ad campaign announcing to the world that they were taking a chance on Detroit, and was doing so much good for Detroit—in 2011, after the automotive industry bailouts and the city was rapidly headed for bankruptcy itself—that it was hiring all these people and making a new assembly line, as if Henry Ford's $5-a-day was reincarnated in the form of watchmaking.

One by one, fashion magazines sent photographers to Detroit to capture this "rebirth" of American manufacturing. On a local level, several up-and-coming Detroit businesses were being hailed as the ones to watch. Everyone was looking for the next Slows Bar-B-Q, a restaurant credited—much to the chagrin of longtime Detroiters—for singlehandedly sparking an entrepreneurial boom in Corktown. On a national level, Shinola was being put in the same conversation with the automakers that made Detroit what it was in its glory days.

You would think that Detroiters citywide would be celebrating Shinola as a success, but you don't know Detroit. Shinola was a darling to outsiders looking in, but was slowly pissing off everyone here in town.

At first, there were complaints about the location. It seemed too easy to set up shop in Midtown, an area where developers, foundations and some government agencies are pouring in the money for revitalization, and not any other neighborhood—especially since there are so many vacant manufacturing facilities dotting the map. Next, there were the prices of Shinola's wares. A watch can cost almost a grand, and a common refrain among social media and comment sections was, "can the average Detroiter even afford a Shinola watch?"

What rubbed Detroiters the wrong way was the very short time it took Shinola to become synonymous with Detroit. Aside from the American manufacturing angle, terms like "made in Detroit"—though the company does not have a union—were being associated with Shinola. And to many living here, Shinola didn't really feel Detroit enough. Unlike Vernors, which has been in existence for a century, Shinola just got here. It's like going from basic training to commander of the unit in a week; Shinola didn't seem like it had earned its stripes.

Anyone opening a business should be aware that they'll meet with some resistance if they try to build a brand on the back of Detroit's comeback, or the city's heritage in general, the charisma and mystique that makes this city what it is. Rookie business owners are either going to have to develop some tough skin if they're going to try to make it here, or develop a skin porous enough to absorb the needs of the community surrounding them.

---

It's not cheap to open a business in Detroit. Despite what you have heard about property values or rental rates, you still need some money. Maybe you've got a nest egg, or maybe you can get a loan. Let's hope you've got a nest egg, because at the moment, commercial lending is very difficult in Detroit because, despite the redevelopment hype, many banks do not see this city as a valuable investment.

If those options don't work, you can jump on Detroit's hottest trend: crowdfunding. Anything is possible with the internet, and that includes asking strangers for money to fund your pipe dreams. Detroit's most famous crowdfunding story is the hundreds of people who donated to erect a statue of RoboCop, the fictional sci-fi officer, somewhere in the city. (As of writing, the statue has been cast, but it has not been placed anywhere.) After RoboCop, it's like everyone decided that crowdfunding is one of the better ways to get a business going in Detroit.

Here's the thing about crowdfunding in Detroit, though: You're asking for handouts in a city with thousands of poor residents. And even the newer residents aren't all that wealthy. What kind of precedent does it set when a newbie can come into town and ask for money when so many people around here are struggling? I mean, I'm not saying don't do it; the struggles of others aren't going to get in the way of your business aspirations. But be prepared for the sting of judgment, and be prepared to rely on out-of-town donors.

Then there are the things people are actually crowdfunding for. A RoboCop statue is decidedly the very least of Detroit's needs. Some people tried to argue that it would draw tourists, thus boosting the city's economy, but if that were true, the goddamn thing would be put up somewhere by now. But there is criticism from locals about crowdfunding ideas that may not necessarily help Detroit in the long run. Raising money for a tutoring program that can teach illiterate citizens how to read? Sure, why not? Raising money for an artisanal muffin-delivery service that only delivers in an increasingly pale neighborhood? Uh…

And then there's this whole notion that crowdfunding is the easy way into business, as opposed to the old-fashioned way of building from the ground up like so many Detroit business owners have done in the past. Not everyone thinks it's fair, so be prepared for that as well.

---

Godspeed to anyone who tries to go the traditional route to opening a business in Detroit. At the moment, it's not an easy process.

You will have to receive multiple permits from the city, depending on the business model. A restaurant, for example, will need a food permit. There may be permitting required from the state of Michigan as well – especially if liquor is involved. Buying the building or renting the space is always easy. Getting up and running with the paperwork is the real challenge.

There are horror stories coming out of the city of Detroit daily. Structures being demolished that aren't supposed to be demolished. Fines imposed on businesses for hanging banners on their storefronts when it's technically against the law to hang a banner on your storefront—and, who knew? Fines being imposed when street art is mistaken for graffiti—building owners are asked to rectify graffiti, as it's an eyesore, but some institutions have been fined after commissioning actual artists to paint graffiti-inspired murals. It's a clusterfuck.

Fortunately there are initiatives with the current city administration aimed at making opening a business easier. The amount of red tape involved is going down fast—maybe not fast enough, or maybe too fast? Basically, no city department is on the same page with anything at the moment.

---

In Detroit, there are several grants, incubators, and competitions that can help ambitious would-be business owners get a leg up in setting up shop.

Competitions are where business owners go head-to-head with other business owners for funding; many of these competitions rely on votes from the public on their favorites, *American Idol*-style. Grants operate similarly, in that there are limited amount of funds available for many people competing, but winners are determined by a governing board rather than the public.

As Detroit redevelops, its incubator scene increasingly flourishes. Incubators help entrepreneurs navigate the tricky waters of opening a business, guiding them toward funding sources, helping with staffing needs and other logistics. They are like the fairy godmothers of Detroit business; they can wave the magic wand a few times to get you going, but it's up to you to go the rest of the way.

Do keep in mind some incubators have better track records than others, and ultimately the onus falls on the business owner to attract a clientele and maintain it. But here's a list of incubators that can help you get started:

## TECHTOWN

**WHAT IT DOES:** Helps connect burgeoning entrepreneurs and established business owners with the resources they need to get off the ground.
**WHEN ESTABLISHED:** 2008
**WEBSITE:** techtowndetroit.org

## REVOLVE DETROIT

**WHAT IT DOES:** Places hopeful entrepreneurs and artists into vacant storefronts across Detroit.
**WHEN ESTABLISHED:** 2013
**WEBSITE:** revolvedetroit.com

## THE BUILD INSTITUTE

**WHAT IT DOES:** Connects entrepreneurs and business owners with a wide network of resources in the city.
**WHEN ESTABLISHED:** 2012
**WEBSITE:** buildinstitute.org

## DETROIT CREATIVE CORRIDOR

**WHAT IT DOES:** Delivers economic resources to Detroit's creative community.
**WHEN ESTABLISHED:** 2010
**WEBSITE:** detroitcreativecorridorcenter.com

## GREEN GARAGE

**WHAT IT DOES:** Supports businesses with an eye toward sustainable development
**WHEN ESTABLISHED:** 2011
**WEBSITE:** greengaragedetroit.com

## BIZDOM

**WHAT IT DOES:** An arm of Dan Gilbert's Rock Ventures, Bizdom offers $25,000 in startup funding in exchange for 8% equity of new businesses.
**WHEN ESTABLISHED:** 2012
**WEBSITE:** bizdom.com

## BAMBOO DETROIT

**WHAT IT DOES:** Provides workspace, resources, and networking for local creative.
**WHEN ESTABLISHED:** 2014
**WEBSITE:** bamboodetroit.com

## GRAND RIVER WORKPLACE

**WHAT IT DOES:** Provides shared workplace and a pop-up venue for entrepreneurs in the Grandmont-Rosedale neighborhoods.
**WHEN ESTABLISHED:** 2014
**WEBSITE:** mygrandmontrosedale.org

## PROSPERUS DETROIT

**WHAT IT DOES:** Seeks to revitalize low-income, minority, or immigrant neighborhoods through enterprise.
**WHEN ESTABLISHED:** 2010
**WEBSITE:** prosperusdetroit.org

## CENTRAL DETROIT CHRISTIAN COMMUNITY DEVELOPMENT CORPORATION

**WHAT IT DOES:** A faith-based economic developer supporting central Detroit.
**WHEN ESTABLISHED:** 1994
**WEBSITE:** centraldetroitchristian.org

## SOLO AND SMALL FIRM INCUBATOR PROGRAM

**WHAT IT DOES:** A program for University of Detroit Law School graduates who seek to help low-to-moderate-income clients.
**WHEN ESTABLISHED:** 2014
**WEBSITE:** law.udmercy.edu

## GRAND CIRCUS

**WHAT IT DOES:** Helps connect tech companies with newly skilled workers; as well as acts as a coworking space for tech entrepreneurs.
**WHEN ESTABLISHED:** 2013
**WEBSITE:** grandcircus.co

## PONYRIDE

**WHAT IT DOES:** Seeks to solve problems related to ongoing crises in Detroit, as well as provides a coworking space.
**WHEN ESTABLISHED:** 2011
**WEBSITE:** ponyride.org

## DETROIT KITCHEN CONNECT

**WHAT IT DOES:** Helps Detroit food entrepreneurs find available commercial kitchens.
**WHEN ESTABLISHED:** 2014
**WEBSITE:** detroitkitchenconnect.com

### FOODLAB DETROIT

**WHAT IT DOES:** Helps small food businesses “grow and experiment” in and around the city.
**WHEN ESTABLISHED:** 2011
**WEBSITE:** foodlabdetroit.com

### SPACE

**WHAT IT DOES:** Solves design challenges while also pushing forth new innovation, as well as identifying opportunities to launch “commercially viable products.”
**WEBSITE:** aspacefordesign.com

### BLACKSTONE LAUNCHPAD

**WHAT IT DOES:** Offers support to innovators, inventors, and entrepreneurs at Wayne State University.
**WHEN ESTABLISHED:** 2010
**WEBSITE:** blackstonelaunchpad.wayne.edu

### WORK/SHOP

**WHAT IT DOES:** Seeks to mobilize entrepreneurs by witnessing other start-ups in action.
**WHEN ESTABLISHED:** 2015
**WEBSITE:** workshop.iamyoungamerica.com

## HOW TO EAT IN DETROIT WITHOUT BEING A JACKASS

They say Detroit is undergoing a restaurant boom, which is true. New places crop up on a near-weekly basis, breaking our pockets as we figure out which new dish is best. Where things get lost among newcomers is that Detroit didn’t have fine dining—or any dining—at all prior to these spots opening up. Let’s get one thing straight: Before these new restaurants came, you could always eat well here.

We're also living in a time where a restaurant's reputation can be broken with a few negative reviews online. Most chefs mean well, and the restaurant staffers will be bending over backward to keep your business. Here are a few tips for how not to be a jackass in restaurants:

1. Never go to a restaurant during its opening week. Wait at least a month before visiting. The order of patrons goes like this in opening week: Die-hard foodies during the soft opening; young, suburban crowds in the first few days; curious seniors in the next few days, and everyone else after. You'll want to be part of "everyone else" when the staff knows how to handle large crowds.

2. Speaking of large crowds, don't expect speedy service. Many of Detroit's new restaurants specialize in intricate cuisine, meaning food prepared fresh for each and every dish. Cooks and servers never have the menu down pat in the first few days of opening, and when they finally do, you're still not going to get an Applebee's experience, since places like Applebee's basically serve reheated frozen food. Patience is key.

3. Beware of peak dining hours, and especially beware of game days. Three major sports teams play downtown, which means many downtown restaurants are crowded before and after. Restaurants near concert venues are also packed whenever a big act is in town.

4. Before you write that awful Yelp review, give the place a second chance. I like to give places a second or third time to get it right, because you never know what might happen. The server is having a bad day, the cook ran out of a certain item. Things happen that are beyond the staff's control. Now of course if service or food quality is consistently bad, Yelp away.

5. Tip well. This should go without saying, but many restaurants make it a goal to hire within the city. Tipping well goes toward the wages of your fellow Detroit residents trying to contend with things like high car insurance, property taxes, rising rents, childcare costs, and other expensive necessities.

6. Tell a friend. Not everyone reads *Eater* or *Hour Detroit*; there are places new and old, big and small, that largely subsist on word of mouth. It's also the best way, in my opinion, to discover something you haven't tried.

7. Remember, nothing is hidden – you just didn't know about it. Calling a restaurant a "hidden gem," a "diamond in the rough" or some other terminology when the establishment has been there for decades just means it was unknown to you until now. Everyone in that particular neighborhood already knew about it, I bet.

8. We're still the Midwest. If a server calls you "honey" or "sweetie," try to resist launching into a feminist rant. It's simply a term of endearment.

## CLASSIC DETROIT DISHES

These old favorites reflect the cultural mix that defines Detroit.

### BATTERED SHRIMP

There's breaded shrimp, the crunchy kind you get at Red Lobster and places like that, and then there's battered shrimp, which is deep-fried jumbo shrimp—real jumbo shrimp—in a softer, seasoned batter. Found at dedicated shrimp joints or as a side order at hole-in-the-wall places, it's a treat with hot sauce, ketchup, or cocktail sauce. You know it's legit when it comes in a red-and-white box covered with waxed paper.

### ASIAN CORNED BEEF EGG ROLLS

There are two restaurants, both called Asian Corned Beef, that serve up what's essentially a Reuben sandwich—corned beef, cheese, onion, dressing—in egg roll wrappers. They're probably neither the first nor the last to do this, but it's a delicacy beloved by those in the know.

## BETTER MADE CHIPS

We have our own potato chip factory on the east side of Detroit, and their snacks have been a staple in school lunches, picnics, and vending machines for more than 80 years. Like Faygo, Better Made has flavors you're not going to see all across the country, which makes them all the more unique. A good starting point is to try the plain and barbecue flavors, then work your way to sour cream and onion, sweet barbecue, salt and vinegar, and red hot. The Rainbow chips, a sweet, crispier flavor, are also popular.

## BBQ ON THE SIDE OF THE ROAD

If you're driving by and see a guy in an apron standing in front of an oil can with lots of delicious-smelling smoke coming out of it, stop immediately and get whatever he's cooking, because it's guaranteed to be the shit. (Though fair warning, we don't really use the term "street food" here.)

## SQUARE PIZZA

New Yorkers have their big, giant slices, Chicagoans have their deep-dish, and Detroiters have their own recipe: cut in squares, sauce on top of the cheese and other toppings, and a crispy crust. Buddy's Pizza is best-known as the purveyor of this style, but other places, like Jet's, Shield's, and Cloverleaf, also have very, very worthy offerings.

## TACOS

Given the city's sizable Latino population, authentic tacos with all kinds of fillings can be found everywhere from fancy sit-down places to corner stores. (Beware that we do not refer to corner stores, party stores, or liquor stores as "bodegas.")

### MAURICE SALAD

Supposedly named after a chef or some other kitchen employee, though no one can say for sure, at the Hudson's department store, a once-mighty, now-defunct chain headquartered in Detroit that was sold to the company that owns Target and is now owned by the company that owns Macy's. (You may also hear talk of "the old Hudson's building," a downtown behemoth that was famously imploded in 1998— it's on YouTube.) Hudson's is gone, but the signature Maurice salad—a salad with sweet pickles, swiss cheese, turkey breast, hard-boiled eggs and topped with a tangy dressing—can still be found on menus in some local restaurants. It's easy enough to make at home if you follow a reputable recipe online; be sure to use one that specifically details the Hudson's origin story.

### BOTANA

Think of it as a Mexican take on the coney. Born in Southwest Detroit, botana is corn chips topped with chorizo, beans, Muenster cheese, avocados, tomatoes, onions and peppers. It's heavier than a typical plate of nachos, and in Detroit, it's an actual dish—not a side or an appetizer.

## THE UNOFFICIAL GUIDE TO ENJOYING FAYGO

Faygo is a brand of pop—not soda—that catches a lot of first-timers off-guard. Most flavors are a little sweeter than bigger brands, though not too sugary. And its wide array of flavors can be intimidating. Detroiters consider themselves blessed to have grown up on Faygo, whose factory is located on the east side of Detroit. It's often missed by expats, who regularly lament the shipping cost of a case of the good stuff. Here's a primer on how to get into our favorite pop.

## REDPOP

Strawberry-flavored pop. The best one.

## MOON MIST

Faygo's answer to Mountain Dew.
Good stuff.

## 60/40

Faygo's other citrus flavor, the answer to Squirt. Good stuff.

## CREME SODA

A vanilla pop.
Unlike any other cream sodas out there.

## ROOT BEER

Some like to make floats of it. Drinking it is best.

## MOON MIST BLUE AND MOON MIST RED

The answer to the respective Mountain Dew flavors. Blue is a bit sweet for some tastes. You can't ever go wrong with Red.

## TWIST

The lemon-lime flavor, the 7UP/Sprite/Sierra Mist of the family.
Best served ice cold.

## GINGER ALE AND GOLD

Ginger Ale is more like Canada Dry, while Gold is more Vernor's. Have to say, the non-Faygo brands are better in each case.

## COLA

Talk to certain Detroiters, and they'll swear the recipe changed sometime in the '90s and that it's not the same as it was back then. Either way, Cola is its own flavor and can't really be compared to Pepsi, Coca-Cola, RC, what have you. Kind of leaves a filmy aftertaste, though. Cherry Cola is a much better execution.

## ROCK & RYE

It's one of the top three, maybe even top two, among Faygo flavors. It's a cross between Creme Soda and Cola, which no one else can really pull off. It's also one of Faygo's best mixers, if you like your drinks a little harder.

## DR. FAYGO

AKA the Dr Pepper of the family. Dr Pepper is better.

## ORANGE, PINEAPPLE, PINEAPPLE WATERMELON, BLACK CHERRY, PEACH, CANDY APPLE

All self-explanatory. Pineapple is a surprisingly good pop flavor. Peach is a Detroit favorite, and a shocker for those who didn't know soda could come in this flavor.

## DIET CHOCOLATE CREAM PIE

DON'T. An awful flavor for everyone unless you have dietary restrictions. Which, even then, just get water instead.

*I'm from*

**JOY ROAD, EXIT 9,**
**COME UP OFF THE FREEWAY.**

*If you ain't from around here, you better be easy.*

—K-Doe aka K-Deezy, "In My Hood"

# CHAPTER 14

## HOW TO HOUSE-HUNT IN DETROIT

In Lafayette Park and other downtown-area neighborhoods, there is a weekly newspaper called the Monitor that has arts coverage, neighborhood news, and real-estate listings. Usually the real-estate listings are limited to Lafayette Park and other downtown neighborhoods, and for a time, one realtor even advertised condos in Acapulco. But back in the day, way back before the housing crash, there was an insert called "Detroit Homes" that had more detailed information about houses for sale all across the city.

As a kid, this is how I learned about Detroit neighborhoods and housing styles. You'd read about each house and how glamorous they were on the inside: "six-bedroom Palmer Park beauty, with dressing rm., sauna, eat-in kitchen, formal dining rm., billiards rm., Florida porch." My mother and I lived in a two-bedroom apartment off Orleans Street, overlooking what is now the Dequindre Cut—I remember when it was railroad tracks, and my elementary school friends used to joke it was the actual Underground Railroad—and thinking these places seemed like palaces.

Listings for Corktown seemed not-so-glamorous. There was one for a duplex where the old train station was visible in the background. I'm not sure if there's a name for this phobia, but I have a fear of abandoned buildings. I think it started with Northeastern High School; my mother's late fiancée went there, and we'd drive by it sometimes. It closed in the 1980s and was abandoned ever since.

So it's weird to me now as an adult that Corktown took off like it did. Detroiters I know do not want to live around abandoned buildings. So why does everyone want to live there in the shadow of one of Detroit's largest abandoned buildings?

A big buzzword around Detroit right now is "transitional neighborhood." Generally, this is a term applied to neighborhoods either on the brink of resurgence or the brink of failure. The unsaid part of this is that if the neighborhood is on the brink of resurgence, it means there are new people moving in—like you!—that are filling empty spaces.

Remember how huge Detroit is: big enough to hold at least two other major cities in its bounds. Only a relative few neighborhoods are generally described as "transitional" by the urban planner types, but I like to think that every neighborhood in the city is in a state of flux.

It's important to remember that there is redevelopment activity going on all over town, though admittedly not at the fastest rate. Whether it's improving the façade of an aging grocery store, opening a beauty salon in an abandoned space, holding a block club back-to-school barbecue, very few neighborhoods are truly dead. That said, one catastrophic event can severely impact a neighborhood's morale and send residents to...a different neighborhood. Because the city is so big, and there are many neighborhoods to explore, someone that moves may not necessarily go to the suburbs. They may just go to the other side of town.

---

In the dark romantic comedy *The War of the Roses*, based on an excellent Warren Adler novel of the same name, an attorney's wife writes notes to owners of mansions imploring them to contact her and her husband first if they ever plan on selling their home. The couple lucks up and is successful this way.

Funny enough, my mother bought our first Detroit home in a similar fashion. Her friend's sorority sister lived behind a widow who died, and the family wasn't sure what to do with the house. So my mother wrote them a note, left it in the mail slot, and soon after the family sold her the house.

It's fine to use this approach; no one is going to call the cops on you or anything if you try it. But the larger point is, there really is no one way to buy a house in Detroit. Or anywhere! But here, we have a few other options besides the traditional broker process.

Get rid of any thinking that the buying process is any different in Detroit than elsewhere. You will have to pay closing costs and all the other fees associated with a traditional home purchase just like everywhere else.

You may have heard that you can buy a house for as little as $1. Absolutely the fuck not. Get this out of your head now. If you see a listing for pennies, the value is in the land. The house will not only be uninhabitable, but impossible to rehabilitate.

You may have seen that you can buy a house for a few thousand dollars. You absolutely can, but generally it will fall into one of three categories:

1. The house is a foreclosure and the bank is trying to move it off-market quickly. There will most likely be a bidding war, so the listed price will probably come in lower than the winning bid. And it will be a cash-only deal, so be ready to pony up.

2. The house needs extensive renovation and is far from move-in ready. You'll spend more than twice as much bringing it to comfortable standards.

3. There are back property taxes owed on the house, which must be paid upon purchase and which add to the listing price.

There are ways to purchase a home at auction. Sometimes homes and even apartment buildings are listed on auction sites, from eBay to off-brand real-estate auction sites. All I can say here is buyer beware; there are unscrupulous people listing properties in awful condition that look nothing like the photos online.

A safer, more reliable way to purchase a home through an auction can be done through Wayne County or the City of Detroit, a path taken by more than a few new Detroiters.

Wayne County auctions homes that have fallen into tax foreclosure in Detroit and other cities. The auction comes in the fall in two phases. During the first phase, every foreclosure on the rolls goes up; these include everything from rundown shacks to beautiful mansions. The first round of auction is generally the most competitive, because the best-of-the-best properties are listed alongside the lesser ones. During the first round, properties are auctioned off at their current value, and bidding increases from there. During the second round of auctioning, the leftover properties from the first round are auctioned off for $500, and bidding increases from there. Some bidders have gotten lucky in getting houses for $500 and nothing more, and the even luckier ones have gotten one of the nicer properties in the second round for much less than what they would have paid in the first round. Either way, it's all a game of chance and not for the faint of heart.

Wayne County auctions do not allow bidders to see the insides of the homes they are purchasing; everything is sold sight unseen, as-is, though you are certainly welcome to do a drive-by. But keep in mind that foreclosed properties may have tax-burdened residents still living there. They will be either living there until they are forced out, they may be squatters, or they may be just like you: bidding in the auction as well, trying to keep their own house. In some instances, neighbors will purchase a home, become an instant landlord, and keep the existing residents as tenants. If by chance you purchase a home with a stubborn resident, be prepared to take legal action for eviction.

The city of Detroit began auctioning homes through its land bank website, BuildingDetroit.org, in 2014. Most entries begin at $1,000 and increase from there. Unlike Wayne County, the city allows potential buyers to view the home in advance of the auction, which takes place online through the city land bank site and not a third-party auction site. The land bank tries to auction at least one house each day. Conditions of properties vary; some may need extensive renovation, while others may need lighter touch-ups. The ones with the most work needed generally tend to auction off at the $1,000 base. All of the homes, regardless of condition, are required to be rehabilitated within six months. (Exceptions apply to homes with great historical detail or larger homes.)

Land contracts and rent-to-own options are also available in the city—though be sure to investigate to make sure the property has no liens, is legally owned by the party leasing it, and is not in foreclosure or at risk of going into foreclosure. Deed searches can be performed at the Wayne County Registry of Deeds.

## SOME ADDITIONAL THINGS TO KEEP IN MIND:

1. Homes on boulevards and homes on corners generally have higher taxes than other homes.

2. The larger the house and lot size, the larger the property tax. You want more, you pay for more.

3. If there are back taxes or delinquent water bills—both of which can run into the thousands—due on the property, they often must be paid to complete the sale.

4. Many of the same above rules apply to condominiums and cooperative housing as well.

Some neighborhoods, especially Midtown, offer incentives for moving there if you meet certain residency requirements. The state of Michigan offers incentives and financial assistance for purchases in Detroit through its Michigan State Housing Development Authority.

## RENTING IN DETROIT

Renting is fairly easy in Detroit. You will not need an agent to find an apartment, though it will take legwork to find the right property. Sites like Craigslist, Trulia, and Realtor.com are popular with apartment seekers, as well as other sites like Michigan Housing Locator and Rentlinx, a site that began as a startup right here in Detroit. Individual real-estate agencies may also list rental properties on their sites. But like anywhere else in the country, many rentals are found by word-of-mouth. You may try joining neighborhood groups on Facebook, where residents often post future rentals. It helps to talk to people who are always in on neighborhood gossip, too: bartenders, block club captains, community activists, and anyone else who generally interacts with lots of people.

We do not have rent control in Detroit, so keep in mind that rental rates are subject to change after the length of the lease. Renters of houses, duplexes, and flats should also double-check to make sure the property is not in foreclosure or at risk of foreclosure.

Landlords occasionally will give a break on rent if you're willing to front some repair costs or perform the repairs yourself. It never hurts to barter, especially if you find yourself loving a certain location but hating the ugly shag carpeting.

---

Now that you're ready to buy or rent, it's time to go exploring. As we established earlier, you will not be ambushed going into certain neighborhoods. You will, however, need to keep an open mind. A black guy in a hoodie is probably cold.

It is difficult to generalize about life in each neighborhood because it's impossible for someone to live in every single neighborhood —unless, of course, you have a ridiculous amount of money and free time. But what we can do is find you a place based on the style of house, apartment or condo you're looking for. Once you find a place, don't be afraid to talk to neighbors—potentially your future neighbors—about the neighborhood. They can offer valuable insight, into such critically mundane details like whether or not your basement will flood during heavy rains. Join the neighborhood organization or block club, if there is one. Be a steward of the environment, too; the city now offers curbside recycling, which you can sign up for at one of two private contractors who handle recycling for the city (rizzoservices.com or advanceddisposal.com), or drop off recyclables at Recycle Here!, a facility in the New Center neighborhood at 1331 Holden Street.

## YOU WANT: A MIDCENTURY–MODERN RANCH

**YOU SHOULD EXPLORE:** Aviation Sub, a district so named for its airfield history before it was settled with homes. (There are two Aviation Subs, one in Dearborn and one in Detroit on the Dearborn border.) Also look into Krainz Woods, an east-side neighborhood, and other nearby neighborhoods such as Davison. Drive up Outer Drive on both the east and west sides.

## YOU WANT: A THREE- OR FOUR-BEDROOM BRICK COLONIAL, DUTCH, GEORGIAN, OR OTHERWISE

**YOU SHOULD EXPLORE:** Um, every neighborhood in Detroit? Because you'll find no shortage of typical center-entrance homes. East English Village and Morningside, both on the east side, have strong mixes of colonials. LaSalle Gardens on the west side, adjacent to Boston-Edison and New Center, has larger colonials. Pingree Park, an east-side neighborhood adjacent to Indian Village, is also worth a look.

## YOU WANT: AN ENGLISH TUDOR THAT KIND OF LOOKS LIKE THE ONE ON THE CARD FROM THE GAME OF LIFE

**YOU SHOULD EXPLORE:** Sherwood Forest, a distinctive west-side neighborhood that is part of a cluster of tree-lined, solid-brick neighborhoods that also includes. University District and Green Acres, adjacent to Sherwood Forest. A small neighborhood to the east of Palmer Park across Woodward Avenue has some examples as well. Try also some of the streets in Osborn on the eastside, particularly near Kindred Hospital.

## YOU WANT: A LITTLE BUNGALOW OR RANCH, MAYBE EVEN A COTTAGE

**YOU SHOULD EXPLORE:** Again, every neighborhood in Detroit. Being a city for the working class, small houses—from shotguns to those with ornate brick- and plasterwork—are in no short supply. Warrendale, Parkland, Aviation Sub, and other neighborhoods in proximity to the Detroit-Dearborn border have them in abundance in varying styles. Rouge Park, Grandmont, Old Redford, Bagley, Brightmoor, Belmont, Barton-McFarland on the west side. Many, many east-side neighborhoods—Grixdale, Krainz Woods, Conant Gardens, Mohican Regent, Greensbriar, Regent Park—have bungalows galore.

## YOU WANT: A CRAFTSMAN

**YOU SHOULD EXPLORE:** Head to the intersection of Grand River Avenue and Oakman Boulevard, and drive in each direction in a three-mile radius. Plenty of streets in this zone have many examples of Craftsman construction—many in need of rehab. Some examples can also be found in Jefferson-Chalmers on the east side, and in the North End closer to the Hamtramck and Highland Park borders.

## YOU WANT: A LARGER HOME WITH MULTIPLE BEDROOMS

**YOU SHOULD EXPLORE:** Indian Village, Boston-Edison, Palmer Park, Palmer Woods, Berry Subdivision, Arden Park, East Boston Boulevard, Virginia Park street between the Lodge and Woodward—the mansion districts. Though in typical Detroit fashion, one street can be different than its immediate counterparts. In Hubbard Farms, for example, Vinewood and Porter Streets have huge homes that are vastly different than ones a few blocks away. Taylor Street, south of Boston-Edison, has a lovely collection of large homes; its surrounding streets have average-sized homes. Bretton Drive in Rosedale Park has larger homes than the rest of the neighborhoods. The remaining oldest homes in Brush Park, once the city's wealthiest neighborhood in the gilded age, fit this criteria—though rarely reach the market.

## YOU WANT: AN EARLY-20TH CENTURY, "NATIONAL"-STYLE HOUSE, SOMETHING THAT'S UNADORNED AND NOT TOO FUSSY

**YOU SHOULD EXPLORE:** Hamtramck. About 99.9% of the homes in this city are this style: Flat-fronted bungalows and flats with a few columns holding up the upper level and an elevated lower level. Several east-side neighborhoods adjacent to Hamtramck also are versed in this style, including NoHam or Banglatown (both names were recently added to the local lexicon, and may not reflect what some of its longer-term residents actually call the area). Try also Michigan-Martin and other Southwest Detroit neighborhoods.

## YOU WANT: A DUPLEX BECAUSE YOU WANT A TENANT ... OR A FRIEND

**YOU SHOULD EXPLORE:** Specific streets rather than neighborhoods. Many of the city's midsized major streets such as Greenfield, Meyers, Davison, Kelly, Outer Drive on both the east and west side, Evergreen, and

Chandler Park Drive have duplexes; there's no one "duplex neighborhood," per se. Old Redford, West Village, Woodbridge, and Corktown have duplexes mixed in with single-family housing. Duplexes can also found in smaller enclaves like Ewald Circle; it just takes some searching.

## YOU WANT: A FLAT

**YOU SHOULD EXPLORE:** Russell Woods, specifically Tyler, Waverly, and Buena Vista streets, and neighborhoods in close proximity; any of the Six and Seven Mile neighborhoods in proximity to University of Detroit Mercy; about half of Hamtramck, and several streets in Highland Park; many Southwest Detroit neighborhoods; Virginia Park and other neighborhoods adjacent there and nearby New Center.

## YOU WANT: YOUR OWN PRIVATE CANAL BECAUSE YOU'RE A BOSS WITH YOUR OWN BOAT, OR TO LIVE NEAR A BODY OF WATER

**YOU SHOULD EXPLORE:** The Marina District, Harbor Island, and other areas in the vicinity of Jefferson-Chalmers, the few areas in the city where you can own a home with a boat slip.

## YOU WANT: A CHARMING ROWHOUSE, BROWNSTONE, OR TOWNHOUSE

**YOU SHOULD EXPLORE:** New Center, the area so named in the early part of the 20th century because the barons of the time envisioned a "new center" of Detroit outside downtown. Woodbridge has a few rowhouses. Hubbard-Richard or Hubbard Farms—the name changes depending on who you talk to down there—has a few as well, and they can be found scattered across Southwest Detroit the further south you go. Streets off East Jefferson in the Gold Coast have converted brownstones and rowhouses designed to look more like contemporary lofts. Older townhomes can also be found in great supply in West Village and Islandview, and there are a handful of beautiful old condos on Ewald Circle.

## YOU WANT: A NEW ROWHOUSE, BROWNSTONE, OR TOWNHOUSE BECAUSE I JUST CAN'T DEAL WITH SOMETHING THAT'S SOOOOO OLD

**YOU SHOULD EXPLORE:** Brush Park, Midtown, and areas adjacent, where newer condos are in abundance—though snapped up quickly because of high interest in those areas. Islandview and the newer East Village nearby also have some newer construction.

## YOU WANT: A NEW(ER) CONSTRUCTION HOUSE

**YOU SHOULD EXPLORE:** Victoria Park, a community built in the 2000s off East Jefferson Avenue on the city's east side. It's one of the few "new" neighborhoods. There is also a small subdivision near Woodbridge and Midtown with several streets named after Motown stars with new construction. (Sadly, it's not called the Motown District or something similarly catchy.) Newer houses can be found scattered in other neighborhoods, though not in big clusters.

## YOU WANT: TO LIVE IN A HIGH- OR LOW-RISE BUT NOT NECESSARILY A LUXURY APARTMENT

**YOU SHOULD EXPLORE:** Palmer Park, hailed as the apartment district of Detroit. But let's get one thing straight about Palmer Park: it's not, say, a borough-sized area. The square mileage is smaller or about on par with many other defined neighborhoods. That said, it has the greatest density of apartment buildings of any neighborhood in town. Apartment buildings can be found elsewhere, but distinct ones can be found in Lafayette Park, the Gold Coast, Dexter-Linwood, on Chicago Boulevard just outside Boston-Edison, Hubbard Farms, around all the local colleges, and on main thoroughfares above commercial buildings. (Many aren't advertised; look closely for "for rent" signs to inquire within.)

## YOU WANT: TO LIVE IN A HIGH- OR LOW-RISE BUT SOMETHING UPSCALE

**YOU SHOULD EXPLORE:** Downtown. Like any other city, the marble countertops and stainless-steel appliances—and the higher rents that come with them—can be found adjacent to the central business district.

Upscale offerings can also be found along the Gold Coast.

## YOU WANT: A LOFT, BECAUSE LIVING IN AN OLD FACTORY IS YOUR THING

**YOU SHOULD EXPLORE:** Corktown, Gold Coast, and Rivertown, where several older converted spaces are now lofts. Milwaukee Junction, an east-side neighborhood on the rise with some loft space, as well as areas on the edges of Woodbridge.

## YOU WANT: A PLACE TO CRASH WHILE YOU'RE TAKING CLASSES AT WAYNE STATE, CCS, UD-MERCY, OR MARYGROVE

**YOU SHOULD EXPLORE:** All the neighborhoods adjacent to those colleges. There will be lots of flats and duplexes near UD-Mercy. The neighborhood surrounding Marygrove is actually called Marygrove, but has several single-family residences. Wayne State and CCS both offer a mix of older homes in Woodbridge and newer-construction apartment buildings in Midtown.

## YOU WANT: A VICTORIAN, A FARMHOUSE, ANY OLD-STYLE HOUSE, PERHAPS SOMETHING BUILT BEFORE 1910

**YOU SHOULD EXPLORE:** Corktown, Detroit's oldest neighborhood. East and West Grand Boulevard, where these kinds of homes have survived everything – including the big, old Packard Plant, right off East Grand. East-side neighborhoods between Gratiot—especially the ones a few miles away from Eastern Market—and Jefferson are not lacking, and Woodbridge is full of these charming homes. West Canfield in Midtown is considered to be one of Detroit's most gorgeous streets – and one of its most sought-after. So is Pallister Avenue in the New Center area. Some streets in Southwest Detroit, like Central Avenue, also have small collections of older homes. Poletown, an east-side neighborhood between Hamtramck and Eastern Market, is also stocked with older homes, as well as other neighborhoods on the southeastern end of Gratiot Avenue.

### YOU WANT: A CAPE COD

**YOU SHOULD EXPLORE:** Rosedale Park, which doesn't have these styles in abundance but occasionally sees some of the city's few Cape Cods go on the market.

### YOU WANT: A CLASSIC FOURSQUARE

**YOU SHOULD EXPLORE:** Dexter-Linwood and areas adjacent; Highland Park, which has these in abundance, though not all have been kept up as they should; Hamtramck; Springwells and other places adjacent in Southwest Detroit; Atkinson Avenue Historic District and Glynn Court, the two areas sandwiching the Boston-Edison Historic District, which has a few as well. Some can be found in the North End, and some can be found in the newly rechristened Woodward Village, a west-side neighborhood adjacent to North End and Boston-Edison.

### YOU WANT: A 1960S OR '70S BILEVEL HOME LIKE THE ONE YOU GREW UP IN

**YOU SHOULD EXPLORE:** The suburbs, 'cause there ain't that many Brady Bunch houses here. Detroit built and built and built and stopped building right before these kinds of homes were built, and started back up again only about a decade ago. They are scattered here and there; a common explanation, though not necessarily true, is that if you see one of these houses out of place in its neighborhood, it may be because a bigger house was once there and it burned down years ago.

---

## HOW TO LIVE IN DETROIT WITH FIDO

There's no official survey to measure this, but casual conversations with pet owners in Detroit indicate that it's increasingly hard to find pet-friendly residences, especially for dogs. Some landlords are friendly toward cats and dogs under 50 pounds, but there is competition among pet owners to land those spaces. And more complexes and buildings that were pet-friendly are either tightening up breed restrictions, grandfathering in current owners of pets under new restrictions, or outright banning pets altogether. For big-dog owners, there's no one reason why they're not always welcome, but based on what folks are saying many new rentals are recent renovations, and landlords want to preserve their investment, or the pet ban is a preemptive strike against breeds that are perceived as vicious. Dog owners will have to work a little harder to find their perfect home, but the right landlord is always more than accommodating. Some landlords give consideration to service dogs or dogs with special needs.

As with any city, please keep your dogs on a leash. Be careful letting your little guy or gal run free in spaces without boundaries. And for the love of God, please pick up after them. It helps, also, to microchip—a quick surgical process in which a small chip containing your address and other vital information is inserted into your dog—in the event of your pal getting lost. And keeping your dog up-to-date on vaccinations is always a plus.

## THE THREE MOST EXPENSIVE THINGS IN DETROIT

Whoever said living here was cheaper than living anywhere else is a lie. The little, pricey secret about living in Detroit they don't tell you is that while price-per-square-foot is way less than Manhattan, you'll still be paying out the ass for everything else.

### CAR INSURANCE

Detroit has the highest car insurance rates in the nation, and even though there has been talk of alleviating this somehow, they're not going down anytime soon. There are a few reasons for this: One, Michigan is a "no-fault" state, meaning insurance companies pay the cost of an accident regardless of who is at fault. Michigan is also the only state with unlimited lifetime coverage for catastrophic accidents, meaning insurance companies pony up even more. Last, because so many drivers—especially in Detroit—drive with no insurance or false insurance, the shortfalls are made up by increasing rates for drivers that do insure their cars.

Car insurance is a tricky subject in Detroit. The address on your driver's license, car registration, and insurance paperwork must all line up in order to not get ticketed. Because insurance rates are cheaper in every city except Detroit, many residents may live in Detroit, but their actual address on paper is somewhere else. This gets sticky for voting purposes, as state law dictates that you vote in the district where your address is. And, it's technically illegal. As a result, a lot of recent transplants to Detroit don't actually have political power in Detroit. In order to make your vote count, you have to switch all your addresses to Detroit. And that includes paying more for insurance.

## PROPERTY TAXES

The houses may be cheap, but the taxes aren't. Property owners in Michigan pay among the highest property taxes in the nation, and Wayne County residents pay the highest taxes in the state. There's no way around paying the piper; those who become delinquent will go into foreclosure. Those who aren't able to pay in full are allowed to enter into payment plans. Be warned, though, that interest accrues the longer you put off paying the tax. Taxes are collected in the summer and the winter.

1. Five Points
2. The Eye
3. Berg Lahser
4. Seven Mile Evergreen
5. Old Redford
6. Riverdale
7. North Rosedale Park
8. Brightmoor
9. Rosedale Park
10. River Rouge
11. Weatherby
12. Franklin Park
13. Warrendale
14. Belmont
15. Grandmont Rosedale
16. Greenfield Grand River
17. Grandale
18. Fiskorn
19. Herman Gardens
20. Blackstone Park
21. Eight Mile Wyoming
22. Lodge Heights
23. Bagley
24. Fitzgerald
25. Littlefield
26. Grand Meyer
27. Barton McFarland
28. Aviation Sub
29. Chadsey
30. Michigan Martin
31. Springwells
32. Oakwood Heights
33. Boynton
34. Green Acres
35. Sherwood Forest
36. Palmer Woods
37. Palmer Park
38. Martin Park
39. Hope Village
40. Russell Woods
41. Linwood Dexter
42. Petosky-Ostego
43. LaSalle Gardens
44. Northwest Goldberg
45. Southwest
46. Core City
47. Woodbridge
48. Briggs
49. Corktown
50. Hubbard Richard
51. Hubbard Farms
52. Mexicantown
53. Del Ray
54. State Fair

# DETROIT NEIGHBORHOODS

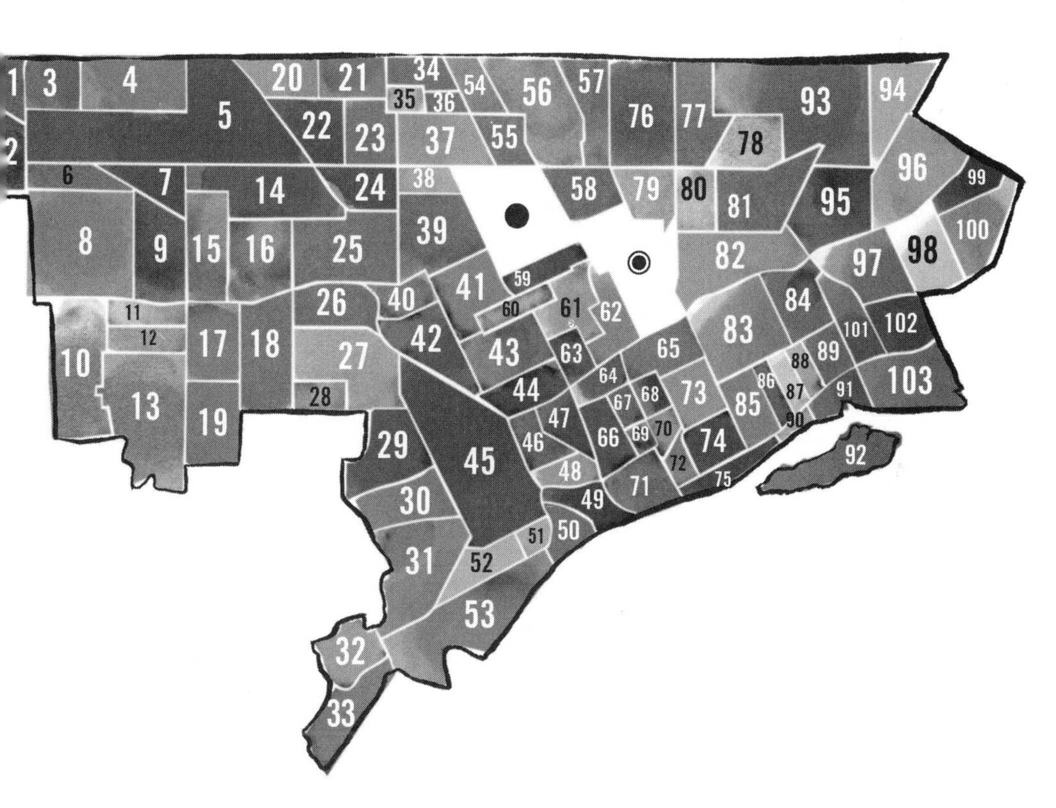


55. Grixdale Farms
56. Grixdale
57. Conant Gardens
58. NorHam
59. Arden Park
60. Boston Edison
61. North End
62. Milwaukee Junction
63. New Center
64. Wayne State
64. Poletown East
66. Cass Corridor
67. Midtown
68. Forest Park
69. Brush Park
70. Eastern Market
71. Downtown
72. Lafayette Park
73. McDougal-Hunt
74. Elmwood Park
75. Riverfront
76. Krainz Woods
77. Nortown
78. Van Steuban
79. Mile Davison
80. Forest Lawn
81. LaSalle College Park
82. Lodgefield
83. Kettering Butzel
84. Brewer Park
85. Island View
86. West Village
87. Indiant Village
88. English Village
89. Mack
90. Gold Coast
91. Marina District
92. Belle Isle
93. Osborn
94. Regent Park
95. Ravendale
96. Yorkshire Woods
97. Chandler Park
98. Morningside
99. Cornerstone Village
100. East English Village
101. Conner Creek
102. Jefferson Mack
103. Jefferson East

● *Highland Park*
◉ *Hamtramck*

### INCOME TAXES

Detroit is one of a handful of Michigan cities to impose an income tax on residents or people who don't live in the city but work in the city limits. Residents currently pay 2.4% income tax while nonresidents pay 1.2%—the highest overall in the state. For years, the city of Detroit was lax in collecting income tax, partially causing one of the many deficits that ruined the city's finances. Since the bankruptcy filing, however, the city is more adamant about collecting, so pay up.

## OTHER PRICEY THINGS

You hate going to Walmart, but a sad truth is that groceries at Walmart in the suburbs are cheaper than groceries at stores in the city. Sticker shock comes in many forms here, and you don't even have to leave the house to experience it. Energy bills, especially in cold winters, run higher than other cities; diligent energy usage can keep a cap on skyrocketing rates. Rehabbers should consider intelligent, eco-friendly modifications, if applicable. Get that leaky faucet fixed, too; water rates are a constant source of squabble among Detroit and its suburbs, with rates fluctuating as the region figures out who should maintain the cost of ownership of the authority.

*It's my house, and*

**I LIVE HERE.**

—Diana Ross, "It's My House"

# CHAPTER 15

## HOW TO RENOVATE A DETROIT HOUSE WITHOUT BEING A JACKASS

When my grandfather was a little boy in the North End, my great-grandmother would take him to the nearby Boston-Edison neighborhood around Christmastime, to see how the wealthy set decorated their houses. He said that he would buy a house like that one day, and eventually he did. In the 1980s, he and his wife bought a home in Indian Village, originally built for Edsel Ford's in-laws.

It is easy to fall in love with Detroit architecture. Because the majority of the city was built before the 1950s, residents are treated to Queen Anne styles in the North End, Tudors in University District, midcentury-moderns on the far edge of town near Rouge River, and Craftsman-style bungalows in deep pockets on the west side. Pewabic tiles, a style exclusive to the pottery house of the same name, can be found inside several of the larger homes in the city; they are easily identified by a shimmering glaze, usually in deep shades of blue, green, or copper. Many homes, big and small, still have their original, solid wood doors, some with stained-glass centerpieces or perhaps leaded-glass paneling.

They are all expensive as hell to maintain.

Anytime I chat with my grandfather, he is lamenting the cost of something that has to be replaced in his old Indian Village house. Because it doubles as a satellite office for my grandparents' business, it must be kept up at all times in case a client visits. They also want to recoup what they spent on repairs, which means investing more than usual for top-notch service. This means things like ten grand to replace a roof, another couple thousand to fix the ancient sump pump. Not to mention scouring hardware stores for replacement radiators, updating the wiring so that the servants' bell still works, and hiring expert contractors to not disturb the integrity of the house.

My partner grew up Downriver and infrequently visited Detroit. I had a hard time convincing him to move here when we still lived in East Lansing. It wasn't until I took him on a tour through Boston-Edison that he decided he wanted to move to Detroit. He was taken aback by the beauty of the homes, and how there were so many of them.

We'd spend a lot of time watching HGTV, which makes house restoration look easy. So when we settled on our first home on Lawrence Street, just north of Boston-Edison, we thought it would be a breeze. It had been vacant for eight years, though all the windows—except for one on the second story—had been intact. All the original entry doors were still there, but the house had still been scrapped of its metal piping and heat registers.

"It's going to be expensive," I repeated several times as the real estate agent, who brought her dog along for protection, guided us through the house.

The living room was covered in aging blue carpet, dusted with leaves that somehow got in the house. The entire first floor of the house was painted the same shade of dull sky blue. The toilets were ripped out of both bathrooms. There were human feces in the master bedroom's closets. There were party beads and handcuffs on the floor of the attic.

But the roof had been recently replaced. The walls were solid. The hardwood floors, protected by carpet for decades, weren't warped or water damaged. There were no gaping holes in the ceilings. And most of the original fixtures were still in the house, including the French doors leading into the dining room, their glass panels still intact. My aunt and uncle's house in Highland Park had doors just like it. So did a townhouse my mother considered buying in West Village.

My partner saw a vision I didn't immediately see, so we paid the asking price of about $6,000. And just like that, we were homeowners with no fucking clue what we had gotten into.

---

When my mother bought her first home, I was 12. We moved to a three-bedroom, 2,800-square-foot home in Russell Woods. The first thing we did was pull up the old carpet, so this is the first thing my partner and I did. I thought because I had pulled up carpet when I was 12 and watched HGTV as an adult, I was prepared for what's next.

You will hear it a thousand times from anyone who has bought a house in Detroit—or really, anyone who has bought a house anywhere—that you are never prepared for what's next. I will say it again. You are never prepared for what's next.

Our goal was to not take out any loans or credit to fix this house. We would live paycheck to paycheck, putting our earnings directly into renovating the house. So my partner and I moved with his mother and worked on the house in our spare time between work and obligations—until we had to move out.

When we moved into our house, we had just barely made it liveable. All the carpet and human shit was gone, electricity had been restored, the piping was replaced. The kitchen had a butler's pantry; we tore that out in favor of making the kitchen and dining room an "open concept," as they say on the HGTV shows. The bathroom in the house was too small, so we ripped out a storage cubby in the hallway to expand it.

We pulled a few Detroit tricks that I'm not exactly proud of. For starters, we were sold a Jacuzzi tub by a guy my partner's sister knew whose house was being foreclosed on. We bought our hot water tank from another soon-to-be-foreclosee. It felt so black market, but I kept telling myself in the back of my head that we're "recycling" this. "If we don't take it, scrappers will."

We took a room-by-room approach to restoration. The bathroom was first, since we needed a place to pee. My partner's uncle is a contractor and he did that for us, ripping out the far-beyond-repair old tile, installing new beige tile, and putting in the Jacuzzi tub, a brand-new toilet and a pedestal sink we bought for 50 bucks on Craigslist. The living room was next. After snatching out the carpet, we cleaned and waxed the floors, took down the mirror over the fireplace (I had to throw a rock at it just to get it loose), skimcoated walls that needed to be smoothed out, painted it, and replaced the floor-to-ceiling front windows, one of which had been converted into a door for some reason.

The bathroom and the living room were the only two rooms that were "done." There was no heating system of any kind, there was still a giant board in place of one of the windows facing the street of the house, and while we had replaced the front door with a more secure door and deadbolt—the door was from Craiglist as well—the side and back doors had yet to be replaced. But our time was up with crashing at my partner's mom's place, so we had no choice.

It was winter when we moved in. We bought a couple space heaters and set up shop in the living room. We slept on a sectional sofa we bought in East Lansing, and used our mattress to block cold air from coming into the arched entry. We had a used washer and dryer for our clothes, and a used refrigerator for food. We cooked on a portable burner.

Yes, there are starving people in third-world countries and shit who have it much worse, but goddamn this way of life was primitive. I hated sleeping on that damn sofa. Hated not having a thermostat at my fingertips to turn up or turn down the heat. Hated the risk of having one of those space heaters set our house ablaze.

It fucks with you mentally. My co-workers at the time knew we had just bought a house. "So when's the housewarming?" they'd ask. "Soon," I'd say. It was always "soon."

Ever seen *The Money Pit*, with Tom Hanks? This was my life now. Except Hanks' character has tons of money to burn, since he is a New York attorney. I'm a journalist with modest means, and my partner was fresh out of college at the bottom of the career ladder. We lived comfortably in East Lansing. Now we were always broke.

Other friends were buying or renting move-in-ready places, and this is when you start to feel buyers' remorse. Everybody just looked so perfect, with their Art Van sofas and IKEA dinnerware. And here we were, washing our dishes in the Jacuzzi and trying to make half-decent meals on a burner that took forever to heat up a can of soup.

The side and back doors we had yet to replace were unsecure, so someone broke in and stole our TV. And there was no way to figure out who stole it, because at this point, we had recruited a few people to help us with restoring the house, and it seemed like there were people in and out of the house at all times. The guy down the street who could paint. Another guy on the middle block who could do walls. Half the time, it was the two of us doing the work. The other half, we had become friendly with people in the neighborhood, and were paying them to help us out.

As the weather got warmer, we took down the mattress from the living room entryway and set it up in the dining room. The dining room was painted and set up, but the kitchen was not, so we hung transparent dropcloths between the two rooms, meaning we woke up every day looking at a gutted kitchen. Next to our bed was a table, a beautiful table I was so proud of; it was metal with a travertine base and a glass top. In our old apartment, it had picture frames and a decorative bowl filled with rocks from a childhood trip to Point Pelee in Canada. It now held that goddamn burner and canned goods.

When you are constantly broke, not living the lifestyle you are accustomed to (or the one you think you should be accustomed to), and living in a construction zone, tensions flare. My partner and I ended up arguing. A lot. There were times when I'd walk away, going upstairs and blasting the music I loved and knew he hated just to piss him off. "When are we going to be done with this house?" I'd ask, frequently. I knew it wasn't going to be overnight. But it seemed to be taking an irrationally long time.

We finally reached a point where two of the three bedrooms were livable. We moved out of the dining room, and it felt good to be able to hang our clothes in the closet. And then that's when our professional lives started to go awry.

First, my partner left his job, which had for various reasons become unbearable. He started looking for other work but couldn't find it, so he took classes at Wayne State toward a master's degree. With options drying up after a year of not working, he sought out a program in Corpus Christi, Texas, that would give him a rare certification he needed. Only thing is, we'd have to split our remaining income for him to not only do the one-year program, but also cover his living expenses.

I'd gotten a new, better-paying journalism job at this point, but home renovations came to a halt while my partner was in Texas. The one thing we'd needed most, a furnace, had to wait another year—so during this second lonely winter, I'd bundle up each night in our bedroom with two space heaters running as temperatures dropped below zero.

Amazingly, the certification got my partner a few job offers the moment he came back to Michigan. And there was nothing more exciting than the prospect of two good incomes, pushing forward the renovation. But as soon as he came back, surprise!—I was laid off. I'd been employed in some capacity since I was 15. To say I was frustrated would be an understatement.

My sanity had already been tested, but my own unemployment almost broke me completely. We still had no kitchen. The master bedroom hadn't been touched since we took the carpet out when we first purchased the house. There was now a window in the attic that needed to be replaced after it was knocked out by a storm; occasionally a bird or squirrel would find its way in. And there was always the risk of our appliances going on the fritz. The oven had stopped working, so coming up with dishes that weren't pan-fried became a challenge. Sometimes the washer wouldn't drain after its rinse cycle.

We needed the furnace. So I set aside my earnings—a strange juggle of unemployment insurance, and whatever freelance work I could get—toward the costs. My partner's uncle did the work for us, and charged us the minimum. Buying the furnace was one thing. Installing it was another.

I spent a year looking for work before I landed back on my feet. I'd exhausted my unemployment benefits, and while I racked up some nice bylines, it still wasn't enough to push this renovation through. So we turned to furniture—I know, I know—to make our house feel like a home. I scrounged secondhand stores for pieces, eventually refinishing a hotel desk and turning it into a sideboard. I stocked our guest bedroom/home office with a bed set from a late relative, a cheapo IKEA desk, and clearance-table knickknacks from Art Van. There was a dining-room table my partner really wanted, something that was cheaper than any reno job. We kept money set aside, and finally bought it when it went on sale.

It felt backwards, for sure—decorating a home that was still missing so much. It was still all we could do to keep our relationship from going off the deep end. There was the occasional dinner out, just to keep me from becoming a hermit. And I did the grocery shopping, trying my best to keep a balanced budget but stocking our bare-bones kitchen with name-brand foods so we'd feel a little bit middle-class.

---

Our neighbors could be difficult to deal with.

On the left was an elderly man with too big a heart. Rumor had

*'Old Slumpy,' a now-demolished mansion that outsiders think still exists thanks to never-ending viral photos.*

it he used to be good friends with Diana Ross and some of the other Motowners. He was increasingly losing his mind, and sometimes would sit on his front porch singing "Little Child Runnin' Wild" by Curtis Mayfield.

He had taken in his grandson, who was loud, always had friends over, and probably sold weed. (The cars parked outside for just a minute or two were a dead giveaway.) I tried my best to ignore it. "Don't start none, won't be none," is what I told myself. The people passing through weren't violent or dangerous or anything. In fact, the grandson was very friendly, and didn't mind at all the two gay guys next door. Never were we at risk of, say, getting caught in the crossfire of a drive-by, or the police mistaking one house for another during a raid. He was too small time. But he was loud.

On the other side was a pill of a man who used to be an inspector for the city. When people like to talk about the kinds of city employees who get away with things just because no one checks behind them, he'd fit in that category. There were all sorts of rumors about him in the neighborhood; that he was paying reduced taxes because of his city connections, that he'd call in favors with the city to get things done on the house, and that he was needlessly cruel to his ex-wife. I have no way of proving any of those things, but I wouldn't put it past him.

We would always disagree with our neighbor over the ownership of a two-foot-wide strip of land between his property and our driveway. According to the city assessor, it was ours. But according to his records, it was his. My partner thought some bushes would look good in the strip, so we went to Eastern Market, bought a few, and planted them. He protested, and always grumbled about the bushes anytime we happened to share the same space outside. One day, his daughter was visiting him. She decided to dig up the bushes – in hilarious fashion, as she attempted to dig out one at warp speed – which led to us threatening to call the police. She left the premises.

"I told you not to mess with that man," one of the neighbors down the street would tell us, over and over.

The former city inspector bought a house way out in Macomb County and had designs on walking away from his bank-owned mortgage and buying back the house when it hit the market. My partner was always chatty with the neighbor and was well aware of this plan. He suggested that we buy the house, which was in excellent condition.

"Can we afford to?" I asked. This was during my unemployment.

"We have to. It will be a good investment," he said.

I looked at our savings, our income, and our expenses. I looked at our house, which wasn't being renovated. I looked at my job prospects. What the hell are we doing?

My partner works at night so he tracked the daytime activity of the house leading up to its listing. We watched as movers, guarded by a sheriff dispatched from 36th District Court, unloaded all of our neighbor's belongings into a Dumpster. (They broke a window in the living room.) We watched as the water department came to shut off the water. And we pounced when a man in a BMW pulled up to put a "for-sale" sign in the window.

The house listed at $6,000. My partner promised the agent we'd have the money right away. The house was shown twice in a weekend. We gave him a deposit at the end of the week, and closed about a month later. We were homeowners again.

What do we do with two houses, with one that's only half-done?

---

Between the time we bought our first house and when we bought the second, we met a lot of interesting people in the neighborhood.

One of the first was a lady with a thick West Indian accent who lived on Calvert. She had grey dreadlocks and walked through all of the streets with a walking stick. She said she could read palms and see into the future. She found out we were gay, and immediately prayed for us to not be gay anymore. "You don't want to be gay. It's a sin," she said. I still see her every now and then, but not on our block.

There's a woman around the corner from us who is a truck driver. Her son was in the Army, and after returning home from service, was robbed, shot, and killed in front of an abandoned house that used to belong to a doctor. Every few months, she puts up a memorial to her son, sometimes with silk flowers, sometimes with a cross, sometimes with miniature American flags.

Many of the men in the neighborhood are older, quiet, and fastidiously work on their yards. And then there are the few that aren't, the ones that throw parties filled with old-school 1970s and 1980s R&B that keep the entire neighborhood awake, or the ones that hang out at the liquor store all day and night.

One thing everyone shared, though, was the desire for some kind of neighborhood community. There's one woman on Collingwood, at the end of the block, who spoke highly of the way things used to be when the block clubs were stronger. There was a woman on our street who had a bachelor's degree, was a member of a sorority, and worked for Ford, who was interested in restarting the block club on her side of the street.

I am far more reserved than my partner. Early on, I feared running into more people like the West Indian lady, and they would be more retaliatory. My partner is the complete opposite, and has wanted to hang a rainbow flag from the house since we bought it. He, too, became interested in re-establishing a block club—except he wanted to do a full-scale neighborhood organization.

My grandparents often talk about all the things that go on in Indian Village. Indian Village has a garden tour, an annual home tour, a garage sale, and other events throughout the year. These are overseen by various committees all linked by the organization, which encourages members to pay dues. And, of course, it's all strictly bound by the borders of Indian Village.

My partner envisioned the same for our neighborhood. A regular newsletter, weekly meetings, a board, dues paid. I cautioned him in advance. "Those folks are rich. They can do that," I said about Indian Village. "Over here, folks are not just going to give their money to just anybody," I remember saying another time.

"But why can't we be like _________?" he asked. Boston-Edison, or Indian Village is what filled that space. He was right. It's one of those things I look back on, wondering if I was classist. I'm stereotyping my neighbors already, and I haven't even met most of them.

I grew up in Russell Woods, just south of our neighborhood. We had a neighborhood organization with meetings and newsletters and soft rules about what you can and can't do. But I also grew up in Detroit, and I've been surrounded by black people all my life. My partner has been surrounded by black folks all of his, but not in Detroit.

I tried to gently explain that Detroiters are a little different. But were they?

Folks get suspicious when someone new tries to tell them what to do. This is exactly what we were doing. Our first endeavor, after talking with a handful of our neighbors, was to print up a bunch of flyers for a neighborhood cleanup. The cleanup would be a jumping-off point for starting the organization, which we hoped to officially establish during a meeting at a mini-police station in a shopping center not too far away in Virginia Park.

It was chilly the day of the cleanup, in that in-between time where it's not quite spring but just after winter. The meeting ground was our driveway, and I was dispatched to go get doughnuts and coffee for whoever might show up.

More people turned out than I expected. We had garbage bags, but didn't think ahead to bring gloves. One of our neighbors brought two packages of disposable knit gloves – the kind steel and car factory workers use. My partner took charge and dispatched everyone to target points in the neighborhoods: Alleys, corners, and abandoned homes where chip bags, takeout containers, and liquor bottles were piling up.

There was just one thing: my partner had a notebook collecting everyone's names and addresses—"to make it look official," he said.

"And what do you need that for?" one woman asked.

That was the "difference" I wanted to talk about, one of the many differences, actually. The woman did give her address, after some coaxing. But my partner wasn't prepared for her reaction.

At the time, I'm actually not sure who felt more uneasy that day: me, or everyone else. I think, looking back, it was me, because everyone was excited that someone was finally taking the initiative to rally the neighbors.

But there was always that awkwardness of us having just moved in. We lived among people who sent three generations to Central High, the school up the street. If you go through yearbooks in the 1960s, you can see the startling change of mostly Jewish classes to all-black ones. I grew up thinking Central was one of those bad-kid schools where fights broke out every day.

There was a line we could never cross with our neighbors, and we learned that at our first community meeting a few weeks later. When my partner brought up the idea of having everyone follow specific sets of rules when it came to exterior modifications and such, like they do in Indian Village, people were livid.

"You can't just come up in here and tell people they have to live a certain kind of way that you feel is best for them," one of the elders, a police widow in her 60s, told us at her dinner table one day. "You can't just tell people they're wrong just because it's not the way that you want to do it."

There it was. There's the "difference" I was searching for. But it wasn't a Detroit difference at this point, it was a young people-trying-to-tell-the-old-people difference.

I would not say that my neighbors did not want to live like the people in other neighborhoods because that is simply a false binary that is far too easy for an outsider to look into. Because people did care for their houses—individually, yes—long before we came along. The same men who tended their own yards didn't hesitate to cut the grass of vacant houses. Even our city-inspector neighbor maintained the front yard of our house in the years before we moved in.

We just jumped into this whole idea of a neighborhood organization too soon. Ours fizzled out, and it didn't help that our professional lives were in turmoil and our relationship was being tested at every angle. Eventually, the woman that worked for Ford fired up the block club on her side of the street, and they regularly began holding chili cook-offs and end-of-summer parties.

---

I am telling other people not to be a jackass, but I was a huge one myself living in this house.

I was mean to my partner for no reason during our renovation, and I too often tried to clip his wings during the experience with setting up the neighborhood organization. But I'd be wrong if I said he wasn't a little bit of a jackass himself when it came to trying to force his ideas of what a neighborhood should look like on our new neighbors.

I guess here's what I'd tell you if I could do it all again, if you're thinking of either buying and restoring a house, setting up some kind of community group in your neighborhood, or both:

1. Have lots and lots of money set aside before you even go house shopping. I don't regret at all paying cash for the house and not having a mortgage. What I do regret is that we did it all paycheck-to-paycheck, and didn't allow for potential catastrophe or hidden costs.

2. Get the big things done first. Know right away if you want steam heat or forced heat. Don't go a winter living in the cold, if you can't help it.

3. Furniture can wait. We weren't the only ones who had company over and everything wasn't up to par. The nice furniture will come in time. Folding chairs and makeshift tables will do in the interim.

4. Budget for taxes! Property taxes always seemed to creep up on us in the beginning. I'd suggest splitting up each year's taxes into monthly payments.

5. Talk to your neighbors, but don't come on too strong. Don't force anything on anyone. Everyone wants the basics, like cleanliness, a feeling of safety and security, a place for kids to play. But what works in one neighborhood may not work in the next.

6. Be patient, be kind. Home ownership in itself is a challenge. Renovation adds so many unexpected layers, and you will be blindsided when you and your significant other come to an impasse about something. Work through it, but remember why you're in this in the first place. You will have to sacrifice and compromise. You may fight, you may cry, you may say things you didn't mean, you may even separate for a day or two just to clear your head. You can avoid all this by working together, and keeping the end goal in mind.

7. Don't be upset at your mistakes. Spilled paint, hammering your finger instead of the nail, broken glass. Shit happens. Everything can be fixed—or you can pay someone to fix it for you.

8. Get outside help, and don't be cheap. Above all, the house is a long-term investment. You don't want patch jobs to come haunt you years later. There will be things you won't be able to do on your own, and you will come out of pocket to get the best available help to fix it.

9. Relax and take breaks. Sounds cliché, but restoring a house is a marathon, not a sprint. If nothing else, keep some wine on hand at all times.

*Well-known for the*

**PLAYAS AND THE HUSTLAS,**

*and if you ain't one of them you must be a customer.*

—Stretch Money, "It Takes Money to Make Money"

# CHAPTER 16

## HOW NOT TO BE A JEALOUS JACKASS

Once I was having a conversation with a guy who casually mentioned that he owned a warehouse outside downtown. Who the fuck just owns a warehouse? Like, oh, I've got two cats, some houseplants, and *a warehouse*. But here in Detroit, that's the way it is now.

If you travel in enough circles, Detroit's younger population can start to look like a walking, talking version of some annual who's-who list. And because we've established in an earlier chapter that everyone in Detroit is six degrees or less of separation from each other, these particular circles can feel like cliques. Cliques of people who are Detroit-popular, whether because they opened a hot, new restaurant, are spearheading a local movement or—though you should always avoid a lazy Silicon Valley comparison—have launched a successful startup.

Growing up in Detroit often meant wanting to contribute to the city in solitary ways. One good job, one nice house, one nice family. So many others existed in Detroit this way, so this is what we wanted. But not these New Detroiters. Now, everyone is a multitasker.

It is no longer enough to live in simplicity. New Detroiters have raised the bar so high, it sometimes feels like the only way to feel a part of the city is to do the absolute most you can with what's available. And there is plenty available. With property and certain living expenses so affordable, you can build an empire overnight.

Here in Detroit, you can own a business or two and three rental houses, serve on a few boards, have a regular guest column in a local online publication, DJ at one of the newer bars every other Friday, be honored by the City Council with a special plaque, co-host a podcast, play on a soccer team, and still find time to be a consultant on some volunteer something or another—all while blogging about it, or at least keeping your Facebook followers apprised.

Is it enough to incite even the slightest twinge of envy? Yes. Very much so.

Maybe envy isn't the right word. Maybe it's fear. Because one of the biggest fears many native Detroiters have about their city is that they may no longer be special in the city that made them that way. When you see newer residents who just moved to the city snapping up all the best condos, getting the best jobs, living the best lives, you think to yourself, "This was supposed to be us!"

The climb is even more difficult for many black Detroiters. It might be the crippling fear of failure, absent the safety net that so many of our white counterparts rely on. It might be that we were never offered the same opportunities as the kids in Bloomfield Hills. It might be because minorities have twice as much student loan debt after college as white college graduates, meaning that we're more likely to spend half our Quicken and Bedrock paychecks paying off loans rather than paying rent to live next door to Quicken and Bedrock. That's just the point of view from me, a black person who regularly commiserates with other black people.

But no matter what your background is, there's still this feeling of having to run this constant marathon here. Because the ones that are doing it well—you must resist calling them overachievers—just make it look so easy. And you think to yourself, why can't I do this? Why can't I own a warehouse?

There's a quote that New Detroiters like to use that goes, "I didn't come here to save Detroit, I came here to save myself." And there's another quote that goes "Detroit is a city big enough to matter in the world, but small enough for you to matter in it." (Saying these out loud gets you *Good Times*-style applause from eager audiences.) Both these quotes are very you-centric. They lean into that Oprah Winfrey-style of thinking that if you put yourself first, good things will come. Until recently, I didn't know that it was possible to be so selfish, or maybe self-centered, in Detroit. Like I said, I, and others like me, just wanted to be successful in our own city. I don't think anyone ever thought that living in Detroit meant that you had to build a brand around yourself. We were always a community. Now it's every hipstepreneur for themselves.

But here's the thing about New Detroit. According to the rules of New Detroit you are not, by any means, allowed to show any sort of jealousy. You are not allowed to criticize. You are not allowed to ask questions. When a group of hipstepreneurs wants to, for example, put up a statue of RoboCop in a public place, you don't say a word about it. Because anything that even hints at displeasure will simply be regarded as being a hater, and haters in Detroit stand in the way of progress.

New Detroiters think that everyone should be able to pull themselves up from their bootstraps. New Detroiters think that playing fields were always level and that everyone has always had the opportunity to reach the same level of success. New Detroiters think that Detroit was just an empty wasteland for years and years and that every bright-eyed whippersnapper with a foundation grant and a dream is the key to solving all of our city's problems. And New Detroiters don't have time for skepticism.

If you are a newer resident, please ask questions if you feel something's not right, and please don't question your cynicism. Embrace cynicism. Embrace snark—there's a growing chorus of people who are comfortable with mocking establishments. Embrace the idea that maybe everything is not the silver bullet for this city's revival.

I am very slowly learning to get over not just envy, but fear. Jealousy can make someone bitter, and bitterness can make someone a jackass. And as you should know by now, you don't want to be a jackass here. But the way that I am dealing with those twinges is by accepting the fact that Detroit is certainly big enough for someone to pursue their dreams and ambitions, but their dreams and ambitions are theirs alone.

If your goal is to own a house in a certain neighborhood, then do it. You don't have to own multiple houses—unless you want to own multiple houses. If you want to be an artist, be an artist. You don't have to own the gallery. You don't have to be a brand. You can be a well-meaning steward of community in your own way. You don't always have to go the extra mile. You can be comfortable in Detroit. And you can separate comfort from selfishness.

There are ways not to get caught up in keeping up appearances and keeping up with the Joneses. Here are some suggestions:

1. Social media is a lie. Remember, for every glamour shot on social media when someone gets that grant or gets that business loan, there's something there hiding that's not as photo-ready. Be content in your own aspirations.

2. Keeping up is expensive. Sure, if you've got money to throw around, don't let me tell you how to spend it. But one thing about Detroit is that it's still affordable enough where if you have, at the very least, a decent-paying job, you can invest your money into long-term things—retirement, maybe?—and not necessarily rehab an old school or some shit to create a financial cushion.

3. Work at your own pace. There's a little bit of truth in those quotes about "mattering" in Detroit. But making a difference doesn't necessarily mean adopting 12 foster children while simultaneously running a microbrewery. If you want to make a difference in Detroit, don't measure your goals against someone else's. You succeed when you set your own goals and reach them.

4. Don't listen to others' advice unless it pertains to you. Listen, maybe these last few lines sounded a bit Dr. Phil, so maybe I'm not the best person to steer you in whatever direction you want to go in. But I've found that I relate most to those who have been in my position. I wouldn't expect a teacher in a charter school to offer advice to a future landlord, or vice versa.

5. OK, cliques aren't *really* cliques. The circles are small, yes. But that's because people live in a bubble sometimes. No one is going to ban you from the cool lunch table or anything. And there's absolutely no pressure to infiltrate these circles. Just do you.

*The pictures were not pretty, the words were not pretty…*

# BUT IT'S THE TRUTH.

—Bill Bonds, WXYZ anchor

# CHAPTER 17

## HOW TO TAKE IN DETROIT MEDIA

A "good Detroiter" is a well-informed one. The news never sleeps here. There is always something breaking.

There's always crime, sadly. There's political corruption, there's something going on with the automotive industry, there's something going on with the Ambassador Bridge—North America's largest international trade crossing, by the way—there's always something going on with the schools, and there's always some dummy out in the suburbs saying something completely racist or homophobic.

Oh, and there's good news. New restaurants opening, new things going on at the Detroit Institute of Arts, things like that. But many people tend to forget that there are more than a million people living in Metro Detroit. That's more than a million things that can go wrong.

Detroit media primarily covers Wayne, Oakland, and Macomb counties. Coverage extends to Washtenaw County when something scandalous happens in Ann Arbor, home of the University of Michigan, and Livingston and Monroe counties whenever something significant happens there. Strangely, the Detroit media rarely covers our next-door neighbors in Windsor, though if you are interested in news from the other side of the border, there are strong local offerings there.

But because Detroit has drawn international attention over the last few years, journalists from publications all over drop into town to send dispatches back. Some national publications and wires, including the *New York Times*, *Bloomberg*, *Reuters*, the *Associated Press* and the *Wall Street Journal*, have bureaus in Detroit; many of those mentioned primarily cover the automotive industry, but will step outside that coverage for bigger events of national interest. Recently, however, the city has made the covers of magazines and been discussed at length on cable news networks by those only passingly familiar with what's going on here.

They're called "parachute journalists," meaning that they jump into town very briefly, do a hot take on what's going down, and book it on the next flight out. Some reports have portrayed the city accurately. Many have not. Because the city is huge, with a wide variety of neighborhoods and people, it's impossible for a journalist on a quick visit to get the full flavor of what life is really like in Detroit. Many reports tend to use a specific neighborhood or two, usually ones that are severely decrepit, to represent the city as a whole. This has been irritating to those who live in the more stable neighborhoods, as well as raising concern that stories of poor, black struggles are being exploited for sensational headlines.

The media coverage of the city's comeback has also been overly generous to what locals sometimes call "white saviors": the young, white entrepreneurs chosen by reporters as the faces of Detroit revival, with copy often positing that these bakers or jewelry makers or whatever can "save" the city of Detroit. Like, the *whole* city, lock, stock, and barrel. If they're not asked to save the city, they're often juxtaposed against the aforementioned stories of impoverished blacks, sending the message that all of black Detroit is in peril, waiting for white knights to rescue them. Some of these stories may not feature people of color at all.

There is danger in being too informed about Detroit to the point where you can be overwhelmed. Taking in too much of the national dialogue on Detroit can be harmful, because you'll always be looking to criticize what they got wrong. You will get angry and you will tweet their editors about why they fucked up and you'll get upset about it all over again when someone emails you the story a week later asking, "Have you seen this?" It can be unhealthy.

Not that you shouldn't take in the national news, but as a newly minted Detroiter, you'll have to figure out how to channel your emotion when you read or hear something that doesn't match your experience. It's why being informed on a local level is a must. There is good journalism in Detroit.

There have been several Pulitzer Prizes won in this town, and broadcast stations have sent alumni to higher posts in bigger markets. And seeing as how Detroit is one of the newsiest cities in the country, a journalist here has to have strong chops to keep up. This market isn't kind to screw-ups.

They tell journalists-in-training to take everything with a grain of salt; be skeptical sometimes. Readers should do the same. Assume what you read is truthful, but don't be afraid to call bullshit in your mind if something doesn't click. But do stay informed. Do learn about this city from its documentarians. And don't be afraid to pay for it, whether through a subscription or donation.

## ONLINE PUBLICATIONS

### CURBED DETROIT

A real estate site where young white people make condescending remarks about the décor choices of old black people, *Curbed* (detroit.curbed.com) splashed into the local media scene in 2011. The site has rotated editors a few times and was gobbled up by Vox Media in 2013, but has remained insightful (if snarky) about in-city home sales and apartment rentals. But while interesting to downtown employees pondering moves to the central business district, *Curbed Detroit* fails to consistently spotlight, oh, just about every other neighborhood in the city – save for the occasional Boston-Edison or Sherwood Forest post here and there. Your *Curbed* staffers may counter that other neighborhoods are "boring," but to not be a Detroit jackass, you should know by now to respect all neighborhoods. Its restaurant-focused sister site is *Eater Detroit*.

### DEADLINE DETROIT

Originally conceived as an alternative news source that filled in the blanks that Detroit's two dailies left open, *Deadline* (deadlinedetroit.com) now occupies a space as a one-stop aggregation shop for Detroit news from local and national sources. Deadline was co-founded by longtime *Detroit Free Press* reporter Bill McGraw in 2012. McGraw, who at the time was a spokesperson for the software company Compuware, convinced his employer to fund the site in its early years. First offering hard-hitting commentary alongside synopses of original reporting from elsewhere, *Deadline* underwent a staff upheaval in 2013 when it lost funding from Compuware. Now independent, *Deadline* still offers occasional opinion from veteran journalists, but its rapid-fire aggregation tactics have been met with ire from reporters at the more established shops.

## HUFFINGTON POST DETROIT

The AOL-owned, New York-based *Huffington Post* began experimenting with hyperlocal news in select markets, and launched its Detroit outlet (huffingtonpost.com/Detroit) in 2011. Like its parent, *HuffPo Detroit* offered commentary from a variety of writers, specifically focusing on local subjects. With changes in direction from its NY headquarters and also perhaps to differentiate it from the local network of Patch sites, which AOL owned until 2014—*HuffPo* recently morphed from a mix of aggregation and local reporting to reporting on Detroit topics with national interest. A distant cousin in the AOL family tree is *Autoblog*, the car website that holds office space in Birmingham.

## MLIVE DETROIT*

An offshoot of Advance Publications, *MLive Detroit* (mlive.com/Detroit) was designed to be the first online-only publication serving a Michigan city for a company that has paper products in other larger cities (Ann Arbor, Bay City, Flint, Saginaw, Muskegon, Kalamazoo, Jackson, and Grand Rapids). When the site launched in 2009, it added news aggregation (then new to the Detroit market) and original reporting to the sports-reporting presence established by reporters covering Detroit teams for the Michigan papers. Today, *MLive Detroit* leans toward more original reporting and is now a competitor to the daily papers despite having a quarter of those staffs. Depending on which metrics you read, *MLive Detroit* is either the most-read publication in the area (when combined with statistics from *MLive.com*, the online hub for all publications in the state) or at least one of the most-read when compared to competing sites offered by rival broadcast and newspaper outlets.

## MODEL D**

A hub for news on startups, small business, community-focused endeavors, and other new commerce in and around the downtown core. Funded by grants, *Model D* (modeldmedia.com) in the past has been accused of being too much of an effervescent cheerleader and seemingly unconcerned with the long-term effects of what a new business can do to a transitional neighborhood. With increased focus, *Model D* has not only found that balance, but also has positioned itself as a louder voice for neighborhood activists and change-makers alike. Occasionally the publication hosts topical forums on issues affecting Detroiters. Its sister site is *Metromode*, which focuses on Southeast Michigan development across the region.

## MOTOR CITY MUCKRAKER

Founded by Steve Neavling, a former *Detroit Free Press* city hall reporter, *Muckraker* (motorcitymuckraker.com) tracks crime, corruption, disaster, and other fun urban topics. What sets *Muckraker* apart from other outlets are Neavling's fiery opinions on social media, his self-described "passion" for tough subjects, his genuine compassion for sources and subjects, and his involvement in the occasional physical scuffle with authorities or others in positions of power. Despite the unexpected nature of what Neavling's involved in day to day, his reporting has been noticed by city administrators and quietly acknowledged—at least, during drunken conversations at Anchor Bar, a popular watering hole for journalists—as a force by his former colleagues.

# NEWSPAPERS AND MAGAZINES

## AMBASSADOR

A lifestyle and pretty-people magazine published by the scion of a pizza and sports fortune and the son of a former mayor. It leans a little more to the celebrity side of the newsstand, often profiling people from Detroit who've made it big and putting non-native famous faces on the cover if they happen to be in town. A lighter read than some other magazines.

## BLAC**

Formerly known as African-American Family, *BLAC* morphed into a free, monthly lifestyle magazine for Metro Detroit's black residents; the title stands for Black Life, Arts and Culture. It has stayed true to its original roots with heavy coverage of all things family, but also offers a much-needed guide to local black businesses and profiles of leading black citizens. Many local stars on the cusp of fame have appeared in *BLAC* just before blowing up nationally.

## CRAIN'S DETROIT BUSINESS**

A weekly business publication in print with a daily web presence, *Crain's* has proven to be a must-read for Detroit revivalists keeping a close tab on the region's commercial development. It is also known for annually awarding local leaders through several ceremonies and special issues, including "20 in their 20s," and "30 in their 30s." *CDB*'s parent company is Crain Communications, headquartered in Detroit and owner of several business publications nationwide, with titles varied as *Advertising Age* and *Tire Business*. Of local interest are *Automotive News*, which covers the automotive industry, and *Autoweek*, a car enthusiast magazine—both based in the Detroit office.

## DETROIT FREE PRESS

Admired by generations of journalism students as the pot of gold at the end of the Michigan media rainbow, changes of ownership and editorial leadership, as well as the general implosion of the print media industry, have corroded a once-mighty Midwest newspaper into a depleted shell of its former self. The remaining staff have tried to resist influence from its corporate parent, Gannett, which acquired the paper in 2005, but resistance has been futile. Layoffs have stripped the newsroom of institutional knowledge, and corporate mandates have directed journalists to think of themselves as #brands first and reporters second. The *Freep*, as it's known around town, is also known for its continued employ of Mitch Albom, a veteran columnist and bestselling author who was reprimanded for falsifying events at a basketball game he never attended, long before it was in vogue for journalists to actually be fired for such an indiscretion. Despite it all, the liberal—most of the time—paper has won two Pulitzer Prizes in the last decade.

## THE DETROIT NEWS

How much longer will the *News* be around after this book is published? Five years? Ten? The end of time? No one knows the answer yet, and here's why that response is elusive: The *Freep* and the *News* are in miserable matrimony thanks to a joint operating agreement, a relic of print journalism's glory days, when cities could afford to support two or more newspapers. The two papers are in a partnership in which individual ad revenues support the individual owners of each paper. If one paper posts consistent losses year over year, one or both owners of each paper could opt out of the agreement. Having been on the shorter end of the stick over the years the JOA has been renewed, the *News* is at strong risk of...well, who knows? It could go online only, it could soldier on in print, it could be sold to a new owner by its current owner, Digital First Media. A conservative-leaning paper (often the polar opposite of the more liberal *Freep*, though in recent years those lines have blurred), it, too, has borne the brunt of changes in the newspaper industry, ranging from layoffs to the embrace of new approaches in the newsgathering process. But despite its politics and that pesky JOA, the *News* sets itself apart with strong investigative reporting, a commitment to local features and entertainment, and leading sports commentary—all of which would be missed should the paper fold.

## EDIBLEWOW

A food-focused magazine with an emphasis on local eating, *edibleWOW* covers chefs, restaurants using locally sourced goods, and the various movements seeking to improve Detroit-area palates.

## HOUR DETROIT

The society and lifestyle mag of the region, *Hour Detroit* is where to look if you need to find a good plastic surgeon. Kidding! It's not just for that. *Hour*—and its sister mags *Detroit Home* and *dBusiness*—also shine a light on local chefs, designers, and other creatives doing good work around the tri-county area, and often provides informative long reads about Detroit intricacies.

## METRO PARENT

The flagship of Metro Parent Publishing Group, which also owns *BLAC*, *Metro Parent* was born from a working mother's inability to find a comprehensive, regular guide for children's activities in the region. Years later, it's a must-read monthly for parents in all communities, serving as an unsung link between city and suburban families.

## METRO TIMES

The last of the local alt-weeklies, *Metro Times* beat out the last of several challengers over the years when it gobbled up *Real Detroit Weekly* in 2014 to become a "super weekly," a term bandied about at the time. *Metro Times* walks a difficult balance between being a true alternative weekly—needling or satirizing prominent local figureheads, doing hard-hitting investigative reporting, giving exposure to local artists and musicians, providing an unwavering stance on marijuana policy (hint: they're always in favor of legalizing it)—and being a run-of-the-mill entertainment guide with endless photos of fun, young blondes at EDM clubs and ads for escorts in its back pages. Because Detroit is such a newsy town, though, *Metro Times* pages are chock-full of news you can use that would put it above, say, the weekly fun guide in the average Michigan town. Like the dailies, *MT* has been shuffled around to different newspaper chains a few times over the years, yet has never seemed close enough to the brink to actually fold. Its dining guide and reviews are must-reads for those of you who are self-indulgent enough to refer to yourselves as "foodies."

### MICHIGAN CHRONICLE

This is the oldest black newspaper in the state of Michigan, dating back to a time when mainstream newspapers barely covered black communities. In its heyday, the *Chronicle* covered every inch of black life in Detroit, from politics to society to entertainment to civil rights. Veteran staff members will brag that they were the only paper to print during the 1967 riots. Nowadays, the paper has shrunk greatly, but is regarded as a must-visit for aspiring politicians, be they at the city level or the state. Gov. Rick Snyder commented at the funeral of Sam Logan, the paper's longtime editor, that his victory at election time could not have come without the *Chronicle's* endorsement. It is the last of its kind in the city; a labor-leaning black paper, *The Michigan Citizen*, folded in 2014.

### NEW MONITOR

A fun little community paper primarily serving Lafayette Park and the East Jefferson neighborhoods, it's also greatly useful for downtown-area apartment hunters. If you see one, grab it.

## THE NEWCOMERS

### HELL YEAH DETROIT!

A local blog (hellyeahdetroit.com) offering adventurous takes on Detroit, with coverage ranging from new restaurants downtown to lounges on the west side to personality profiles on everyone in between.

### DAILY DETROIT

A local blog (dailydetroit.com) offering positive views of Detroit, geared specifically toward newcomers getting acclimated to downtown.

### INSIDE SOUTHWEST

An online publication (insidesouthwest.com) dedicated to happenings and culture in Southwest Detroit.

### THE METROPOLITAN

The official print newspaper for travelers in the Detroit Metropolitan Airport. Offers longreads about the area and some interviews of interest to visitors.

### DETROIT LIVE

A free monthly print magazine dedicated to coverage of live acts and venues in the region, with a regular spotlight on up-and-coming local artists.

## THE NICHES

### BETWEEN THE LINES

The preeminent weekly newspaper for Detroit's LBGT population, *BTL* features interviews with celebrities national and local, social and political news affecting gay citizens, and is a guide to gay-friendly businesses, places of worship and gay events in the region. Look out for the Pride-Source yellow pages, an annual, more comprehensive list of resources for LBGT residents.

### HAMTRAMCK REVIEW

The community newspaper of Hamtramck with local news and views. Pick it up if you're looking for a place to rent in town; the more elusive listings can be found here.

### LATINO

A weekly Spanish-language publication distributed in Southwest Detroit.

### DETROIT JEWISH NEWS

The community link between Detroit's expansive Jewish community in the tri-county area. Occasionally offers insight between relations between the Jewish community and other communities.

### NUESTRA DETROIT

A community-oriented Spanish-language paper in Southwest Detroit.

### EL CENTRAL

Another community-oriented Spanish-language paper in Southwest Detroit.

### THE ARAB-AMERICAN NEWS

Found mostly in Dearborn, but also in other heavily Arab communities, the Arab-American News offers local happenings in the Arab community as well as dispatches from the Middle East.

### MICHIGAN KOREAN WEEKLY

Found in Macomb County and other Asian enclaves, this Korean-language paper is one of the stronger Asian-language papers in the region.

### THE MICHIGAN CATHOLIC

Based in Detroit and published by the Archdiocese of Detroit, it offers profiles and happenings from the local Catholic churches.

# RADIO AND TV STATIONS

## WWJ (950 AM)

All news, all the time – except when there's a big game on. WWJ offers solid radio reporting in an age when radio news is becoming obsolete, and it regularly reigns in local ratings. As a CBS Radio affiliate, WWJ also benefits from streaming breaking news from other parts of the country as it happens. If you're a driver, keep WWJ as a preset, as they are always on top of traffic situations on the roads.

## WJR (760 AM)

Half conservative news, half talk radio, and stomping grounds for some of Detroit radio's most venerable talkers. Generations of listeners know WJR as the home of the legendary J.P. McCarthy, a hard-hitting host who is regarded as one of the best, if not the best, radio news personalities in the Motor City. The right-leaning views of some hosts clash with some listeners (and they do syndicate a lot of national right talk, including Rush Limbaugh), but politicians, business executives, and other local leaders often are chatty with hometown hosts, particularly morning host Paul W. Smith.

## WDET (101.9 FM)

Detroit's public radio station based out of Wayne State University is a regional force thanks to its commitment to both local news reporting and commentary and local music. Depending on who you talk to, listeners are either tuned into lively panel discussions in the morning with local big names, or they are hooked on the wide variety of nighttime music programming, which includes Detroit hip-hop, alternative, jazz, classical, and just about every other genre. Being a public radio station, WDET is also home to national NPR programming, but the focus on local music differentiates it from other Michigan NPR affiliates. You'll want to be a donor.

## WCHB (1200 AM)

Owned by Radio One, which has a portfolio of urban radio stations nationwide, WCHB is essentially news and talk for Metro Detroit's black population. Oh, that doesn't mean it's only for black people, but the issues discussed tend to affect the black community. Longtime radio presence Mildred Gaddis is an anchor of the station, and her interviews with local leaders are a must-listen regardless of your background.

## WDTK (1400 AM)

A Fox News affiliate that leans heavily into conservative and religious talk. Formerly a black religious station with deep hometown roots (it was owned by a lively personality named Martha Jean "The Queen" Steinberg, one of Detroit's most outsized personalities, and one of the few black women to ever own a radio station), most of WDTK's programming is now syndicated from elsewhere.

*Mort Crim, former WDIV anchor and source of inspiration for Will Farrell's Ron Burgundy.*

## WDIV (CHANNEL 4)

NBC affiliate home to Carmen Harlan, the queen of local TV news and arguably one of the area's most recognizable faces. Harlan paired with broadcaster Mort Crim—known to some as a newsman, others as a voice on a White Stripes album—for years until his retirement and now delivers evening broadcasts with the formidable Devin Scillian. WDIV also has rights to broadcast America's Thanksgiving Parade, a local tradition for decades that's a must-watch each year. (But you should go to the parade in person if you can!) Because Harlan, Scillian, and other longtime vets have the longest familiarity with viewers, WDIV is often the highest-ranked TV station in the market. It's mostly straightforward news with no gimmicks (except around sweeps weeks), but its morning and afternoon programming is decidedly more lighthearted.

## WXYZ (CHANNEL 7)

An ABC affiliate increasingly known among Detroiters for its former anchors rather than its current ones. WXYZ was the home of Bill Bonds, one of the last of the old-school TV newsmen who told it straight on air, often injecting his own views into otherwise rudimentary reporting. In recent years, WXYZ has positioned itself as more of a community-oriented station with initiatives like "Detroit 2020," which focuses on the region's evolution, and strong investigative reporting into local and suburban politicians and businesses. WXYZ often breaks big news locally, but is sometimes hampered by sensational, breathless presentation.

## WJBK (CHANNEL 2)

Fox affiliate that looks nothing like Fox News, but everything like Detroit: unpredictable and wildly experimental. "Fox 2" has hired reporters and commentators without news broadcasting backgrounds—including Pulitzer-winning reporters Charlie LeDuff and M.L. Elrick, and Charlie Langton, an attorney with a distinguishably loud, adrenaline-soaked voice—to deliver the kinds of stories not always seen on competing stations. Its morning and evening programming couldn't be more opposite. In the mornings, anchors and reporters deliver a softer version of *Good Morning America* or *Today*. At nights, WJBK broadcasts *The Edge*, longer looks at newsworthy items, and *Let it*

*Rip*,*** a panel discussion covering hot-button local issues with guests from the political, civic or religious realms. If you're into black preachers getting in yelling matches with wealthy white businessmen about gentrification and other sensitive racial issues, *Let it Rip* is for you—but all panelists are going to say at least one thing you're thinking.

## WADL (CHANNEL 38)

Not much news here except for brief updates in between programming. However, WADL is known for two things: Being one of the last independently owned stations in the region, and for airing reruns of popular sitcoms you can't otherwise get without a cable package.

## WMYD (CHANNEL 20)

The MyNetworkTV affiliate, WMYD currently carries some evening news programming produced by WXYZ. Over the years, WMYD has taken on many forms, from being a carrier of local-affairs programming to serving as a rerun warehouse.

## WTVS (CHANNEL 56)

Detroit's PBS affiliate, but also an outlet for some local commentary, including *MIWeek*, a newsmagazine examining statewide and city issues from the perspective of Detroit journalists. WTVS also regularly airs a wide array of local programming, ranging from regular local features to one-off documentaries and other productions. Like WDET, keep your wallets open wide during pledge drives; it's worth it.

## WKBD (CHANNEL 50)

Once a broadcaster of Detroit's only 10 p.m. newscast way back in the day. Now a CW affiliate, WKBD carries no local news, but, hey—CW!

* *I used to work here.*

** *I freelanced a few pieces here.*

*** *I don't smoke weed, but I've been told if you get baked while watching* Let it Rip, *you'll learn more about Detroit than reading every book on the subject, including this one.*

# WHAT YOU LEARN ABOUT DETROIT ON THE SMALL SCREEN

There are lots of movies set in Detroit, like *Sparkle*, *Dreamgirls*, *Four Brothers*, and, of course, *RoboCop*. And then there are popular movie characters from Detroit, chief among them Axel Foley of *Beverly Hills Cop*. But there isn't a quintessential Detroit movie, really. *Gran Torino* came pretty close, but that's about it. *Mr. Mom*, in which Michael Keaton played a laid-off auto engineer, offered some peeks into the industry, but not a lot about the city. Some of the best fictional depictions of Detroit that actually mirror real life here have been on TV. And then there were the shows that weren't even close.

## MARTIN

This Martin Lawrence vehicle than aired for five seasons in the 90s is hands-down the greatest show to ever take place in Detroit, despite none of its cast members having origins here. It edges *Home Improvement* out slightly for a few reasons. *Martin* used exterior shots of actual Detroit landmarks—specifically Garden Court Apartments, where the main character lived—and occasionally worked in Detroit locations in its dialogue. The characters were huge fans of local sports, including the Pistons. And while *Home Improvement* felt more like a dedication to Michigan, there was no ambiguity about where *Martin* was set, as almost every episode mentioned the city's name at least once.

## HOME IMPROVEMENT

Tim Allen gets major props for rocking a sweatshirt from a Michigan college in every episode, and even more props for being a major gearhead living in the Motor City. But is it as memorable as other sitcoms from this era? Talk to anyone who watched *Home Improvement* back in the day, and other than Al Borland's plaid shirts, the default "what do you remember most" answer is JTT—that's teen idol Jonathan Taylor Thomas, for the old heads.

## SISTER, SISTER

If you were to rank the top 10 black sitcoms of the 1990s, *Sister, Sister*, starring Tia and Tamera Mowry as separated-at-birth twins who find themselves reunited under one roof, would probably come in at number 11, if we're being honest. It was, however, one of the few 1990s shows to depict Detroit in a positive light. It showcased black wealth and entrepreneurship, healthy family dynamics, academically minded students, and no one was shot. There were certain "Detroit" elements missing, though; I don't recall a single episode where the Mowry twins were doing footwork to a ghettotech mix.

## DETROIT 1-8-7

They tried with this one. Doomed from the Atlanta-filmed premiere episode that looked nothing like Detroit, this was one crime drama that never seemed to get it right. TV critics felt it to be a cheap re-do of *The Wire*, but locals criticized the show's authenticity—including a major groaner when a character said "soda" instead of "pop." It was canceled after one low-rated season, and series co-star James McDaniel penned a heartfelt letter to the city of Detroit thanking residents for their hospitality.

## LOW WINTER SUN

Another Detroit cop show that didn't find its audience, *Low Winter Sun* was patterned after a UK series of the same name. UK-to-US doesn't always translate, and although *Sun* was far more ambitious than *1-8-7*, it, too, felt like *The Wire*-lite and was canceled after one season.

## FREAKS AND GEEKS

Lots of people forget this one-season cult classic was set in a fictional Detroit suburb. Chippewa, MI, is not a real place. Chippewa Valley High School in Clinton Township, however, is, and the blandness of suburbia reflected in *Freaks* isn't all too much different than how Clinton Township really is.

### HUNG

Filmed in the Detroit suburbs, *Hung* followed the misadventures of a high school basketball coach with a large dick who turns to prostitution to make ends meet. At the time of its announcement, its risqué plot raised eyebrows among the locals. Now, it's just another one in a long line of HBO's adult-themed shows that was critically acclaimed, but didn't quite reach the popularity of, say, *Sex and the City* or *Six Feet Under*.

### HONORABLE MENTIONS: SOUL MAN and UNDATEABLE

Two relatively newer Detroit-set shows whose legacies are too early to determine. You know how quickly shows are canceled and forgotten these days.

## THE BIGGER SCREEN GEMS

When Detroit hit bottom in 2009 and again in 2013, documentary filmmakers couldn't get here fast enough to document tales of woe and despair—mixed in with the eternal optimism of young white people, of course. There are countless documentaries out there, but here are some that hit the mark, as well as some that have nothing to do with the city's current problems at all.

### DETROPIA

This 2012 documentary followed working-class residents, politicians and other locals after the 2009 automotive industry crash, but before the city officially filed bankruptcy. It was gripping, it was heart-wrenching, but…well, I won't spoil the ending. But many viewers had mixed feelings about it.

### BURN

This film explored the grueling, day-to-day lives of Detroit firefighters working to put out an increasing number of fires with a decreasing amount of resources.

## THE JITTERBUGS: PIONEERS OF THE JIT

Many major cities have their respective street dancing styles, but the intricate footwork of "jit," born from Detroit street gangs and evolved alongside the city's techno scene is unlike any other. As this doc shows, it's a dance that everyone in Detroit knows and fortunately hasn't been duplicated elsewhere.

## STANDING IN THE SHADOWS OF MOTOWN

The story of the Funk Brothers, Motown's backing band, remained untold until this heralded film was released, finally shining a light on how Berry Gordy built an empire on rhythms honed in local jazz clubs. Some of the Funk Brothers passed away after this film was released, and as many of Motown's remaining stars age, this is now an ever-increasing important link between Detroit's music past and present.

## REQUIEM FOR DETROIT?

Another gloomy doc, this doc explored the rise and fall of the city during the height of the 2009 automotive collapse from a British point of view.

## THE FAB FIVE and BAD BOYS

Both these films—one tracking the legendary University of Michigan basketball recruiting class, the other focusing on the Detroit Pistons' epic '80s-'90s run—are among the finest in ESPN's "30 for 30" documentary catalogue.

*There wasn't very many places you could go when I came to Detroit,* **UNLESS IT'D BE SOMEBODY'S HOME.**

—Ruth Ellis, LGBT rights activist

# CHAPTER 18

## HOW TO BE GAY IN DETROIT

A quick note on gayborhoods in Detroit: There are none! There are gays and lesbians, and there are neighborhoods, and there are gays and lesbians in neighborhoods, but if you're looking for something akin to Boystown or the Castro, it's not here.

There is Ferndale, an extremely gay-friendly city that elected Michigan's first openly gay mayor. But it's a suburb on the Eight Mile border. In Detroit proper, gay and lesbian life is scattered in different pockets with not much cohesion.

Maybe I shouldn't say that. There is Palmer Park, which likes to think of itself as a gayborhood. Palmer Park is an apartment district in the north-central part of the city, just south of Ferndale but north of Highland Park—a city within Detroit. In the 1960s, '70s, and '80s, it was a magnet for gays and creatives alike, with beautiful, spacious apartments adjacent to one of the city's largest parks. Through the '90s and 2000s, Palmer Park went through a downturn, with several of the high-rises falling vacant. Still, it is home to a large part of the LBGT population.

What Palmer Park isn't, however, is one of those gayborhoods where residents fly rainbow flags high and there are cute little bakeries in every storefront. In fact, there are hardly any storefronts in Palmer Park; it is bordered by a section of Woodward Avenue that is still recovering from decades of economic fallout.

Palmer Park also is facing a quiet crisis: a rash of transgender murders in the area over the past two years, with no known link between them other than each victim being transgender. Investigators can't say if the attacks are hate crimes, or if they are coincidentally victims of Detroit crime in general. What we do know is that all is not well in Palmer Park.

Not too far from Palmer Park within the bounds of Highland Park is the Ruth Ellis Center, a nonprofit that serves LBGT youth. It is named for Ruth Ellis, an out lesbian in Detroit who lived to be 100 years old, and was a force in LBGT community activism in the city. Head north on Woodward toward Ferndale, and you'll surely be run into the folks at Affirmations, another resource hub not just for LBGT youth, but for gays and lesbians of all ages.

There is exactly one gay bar in Palmer Park: Menjo's, one of the literal handful of gay bars period in the city. Menjo's is the oldest of Detroit's gay bars and perhaps the most popular in the city limits. A few miles away, but certainly not within walking distance of Menjo's and Palmer Park, is Gold Coast, a gay male strip club on the east side of Detroit on Seven Mile Road. Not too far from Gold Coast is Innuendo, an east-side gay club with a mostly black crowd. Oh, a mention of race again! But let's be honest here; if you're reading this and you've got "sorry, not into black guys" in any of your profiles, you probably should know where you should and shouldn't go.

In the Warrendale neighborhood near the Detroit-Dearborn border, Gigi's trends younger with a diverse crowd of blacks, whites, Arabs from Dearborn, and Latinos from Southwest, while Adam's Apple is more of a neighborhood bar for the older set. There's Hayloft Saloon in that area as well, a bear and daddy hangout. And then there's the Woodward, which straddles the border of Detroit's North End and New Center neighborhoods. White gays call it "the Hoodward" because it's the center of black gay life in the city.

I don't mind the Woodward, although a story I like to tell is that one of the times I was there, several of the patrons decamped to the coney island across the street at the club's closing time, a fight broke out, and someone was shot. That doesn't happen every night, obviously. But shit gets real sometimes. The Woodward, however, does seem to attract a few C-list and B-list out celebrities, reality show stars, and the occasional R&B singer. As I write, Jussie Smollett of *Empire* fame made a surprise appearance there recently.

Looking for a lesbian bar? Forget it—there are none in the city. At least not now.

In short, there are fewer gay bars in Detroit than there are in gayborhoods nationwide. Some bars try gay nights once a week to varying success, and there have been failed attempts to open other fully gay bars outside the regular places; I once attended the opening of a bar inside an aging strip mall. Being next to a grocery store and a beauty supply, it faded pretty fast.

There are a few reasons why gay life in the city limits is lacking. It could be because of the black Christian stronghold on the city, which either keeps people in the closet or keeps would-be club owners from going after the market because they might be shut down. It could be because Detroit has always been a blue-collar town with not exactly the same kind of fabulous gays you might find in Manhattan. Members of the LBGT community, however, are not nonexistent.

I was blessed enough to know gay men and women early on in my upbringing. My mother worked with an openly gay man and a transgender woman when I was a kid. One of my elementary school gym teachers—a gym teacher, how stereotypical, right?—was a lesbian. It wasn't paradise, though. My mother was friends with a gay couple whose house was burned down just because. They lived in the neighborhood I live in now, though we haven't had those same kinds of problems, fortunately.

As the country increases its tolerance toward gays and lesbians, Detroit has as well. An openly gay man served as city council president in the last decade—though there are some cynics who argue that he was only elected because prior to serving in politics, he was a well-known TV news broadcaster. Still, it was a giant step forward for a city where, in my high school, the out kids were ostracized to their own cafeteria table and the rest of us waited until graduation to come out of the closet.

Perhaps it's not all terrible that Detroit doesn't have a concentrated gayborhood, because since the city has so many historic districts, happy gay couples can be found taking up residence in gorgeous homes, making for a kind of diversity that doesn't have to revolve around class or race. Gay Detroiters can be found in Indian Village, Sherwood Forest, Palmer Woods, East English Village, Boston-Edison, Grandmont, anywhere there's brick and leaded glass.

For walkable neighborhoods—and by walkable, we have to

go with the Detroit definition of "at least two bars and a flower shop nearby"—however, many gays eventually find themselves in the suburbs, specifically Ferndale, Royal Oak, Pleasant Ridge, Birmingham, and increasingly Hazel Park. Ferndale is the gayest city in Southeast Michigan. Royal Oak is where gays with money live. Birmingham is where gays with lots of money live. Pleasant Ridge is, "I like Ferndale, but not that much." And Hazel Park is, "I was priced out of Ferndale." You'll find all of them and more at Pronto! in Royal Oak, the closest thing we've got to one of those trendy San Francisco lounges you see in all the gay shows, or Soho, another popular-kids' place with exposed brick and velvet seats.

The pendulum is very, very slowly swinging toward attracting more gays to live in Detroit, however. Motor City Pride, Michigan's largest annual pride fest, moved from Ferndale to downtown Detroit in 2011. That's every summer, along with Hotter than July, Michigan's largest black pride fest. It does not say "blacks only," but Hotter Than July—always in Palmer Park—doubles as a community event for Detroit's black LBGT community and as an education forum for issues affecting the population such as safe sex and mental health.

Gay men should be aware that just like, oh, everywhere else in the country, the "preferences" are still very strong. If you're white and into black guys, try not to be too heartbroken at the "not into whites" declarations. Same if you're too fat, too skinny, too Arab, too Mexican, too whatever. In short, gays here are just like the gays everywhere else. What probably separates gay men here from other places is that the ones here aren't afraid to get dirty. You'll find gays unafraid to work blue-collar jobs. You might find some gays who've done time. "420-friendly" is also *very* common.

Don't expect everyone to accept you as you are, though. There are many people who are ignorant or intolerant. Somebody's auntie is probably going to try to pray over you if they find out you're gay. Rarely do situations escalate into violence, but every once in a while, a gay bashing makes the news. Detroit is by no means a violent place for gays, but there are some small-minded dumbasses out there.

Pride is the key to shifting attitudes, however. I know some gays and lesbians bristle at the thought of conforming to heteronormative standards to be accepted: monogamy, not acting too gay in front of the straights, keeping your private life private and so forth. But when my neighbors saw that my partner and I were just living like a regular old married couple, we didn't get any complaints. Sure, some of the kids had to have some additional explanation, because some of the kids in our neighborhood had never seen a gay couple, no less a gay person period. Once they got it, though, they got it.

If all else fails? Go to Ann Arbor. It's Michigan's most liberal city and therefore more tolerant. You'll have to have a Prius or a Subaru to live in Ann Arbor, though—it's the rule.

*Detroit's where I felt like*
**I REALLY GREW UP.**

—Miley Cyrus

# CHAPTER 19

## HOW TO BE A DETROIT HIPSTER

I like to think of my aunt Liz as one of the original Detroit hipsters. I don't think she'd like to be called a hipster, though. She was just living her life.

My aunt arrived in Detroit in utero and was the first of this branch of the family to be born here. So she fits the "born in Detroit" qualification. She also went to Cass Tech, another mark on the checklist that some residents like to use whenever they want to measure someone's Detroit cred. But even in high school, she was doing things others weren't—or couldn't. Cass in the 1960s had an honors program, and a high honors program. Auntie Liz was one of the first black students to integrate the high honors program.

Liz is one of those girls that'd we'd obsess over now: smart and geeky, yet still cool enough to change the world. But she and her sister, my aunt Jean, had a restless spirit that pushed them to rebel against the status quo. While enrolled at Wayne State (there's another on the I'm-So-Detroit checklist), both my aunts were involved with the local Black Panthers movement, eschewing the Southern respectability my great-grandmother instilled in them. And they both entered into technology majors—we call it STEM now—when women, especially black women, weren't doing so.

Jean married one of those revolutionary, "no Viet Cong ever called me nigger" brothers who came back from Vietnam jaded and hyperaware about conspiracies against the black man. Liz dated, but didn't make marriage a top priority. She played instruments with expert precision—bassoon, guitar, autoharp, cello, piano. She was a Trekkie, watching the original *Star Trek* broadcasts and following every film and TV incarnation since. She studied other religions besides our family's staunch Methodism and other languages. And she drove a Volkswagen with a stick shift.

I guess what would make her specifically a Detroit hipster is that she was doing then all the things that so-called Detroit hipsters are doing now. She had an apartment in West Village, which has different meaning now than it did when she was there. During her time there, when I was little, West Village was simply the village west of Indian Village. There were apartments and townhouses and generally folks just lived. It was a hidden gem, though—cheaper rents than on Jefferson Avenue, yet still having some of the historic prestige of Indian Village next door. Now, West Village is a destination neighborhood for entrepreneurs and new residents, because it has cheaper rents than on Jefferson Avenue, yet still has some of the historic prestige of Indian Village next door.

Liz was always up on the newest restaurants and things to do in the city. The rebellion never left, meaning she was always fully suspicious of corporate influences. She embraced other cultures without abandoning her own. She was probably one of the most intelligent and worldly people I've ever known, and so undeniably Detroit at the same time. She passed way too young in 2013.

Not too long ago, there was an article in the now-defunct *Real Detroit Weekly* about the "rise" of West Village. And I wanted to scream. I wanted to show Auntie Liz the things they were saying about the neighborhood she once called home. The piece essentially said West Village was abandoned (it wasn't) and that it was waiting for new business to spark a fire (that was already there) in the neighborhood. Some new businesses had opened there; they were just short of being called outright colonists. Worst of all, most of the new residents profiled in the piece were white, even though West Village's demographics hadn't really changed in years. *Real Detroit Weekly*'s piece essentially erased the contributions residents had made to the area over the last few decades, including my aunt's. I took it personally.

In Detroit, we're far more prone to give credit to anyone young and fresh because the things they think they're doing are brand new.

They're absolutely not. Humans have been on earth for how long now? There's nothing new under this sun. And whatever these new Detroiters are doing, there are probably some old Detroiters like my aunt that have already done it.

---

I'm a fan of top-shelf cocktails and Chuck Taylors and I'm a Detroit resident. I like live music, and I tend to know about new art galleries before the rest of my friends. Could I be a hipster? Maybe. I'm not quite sure.

One of the consequences of the collapse of journalism here in Detroit is that newsrooms gutted of their diversity in age and race are left with veterans forced to guess at the habits of their grandchildren's generation, and younger, green journalists who haven't figured out how to communicate with people that aren't just like them. And that's a given anywhere, not just Detroit.

Here in Detroit, many people rely on the big outlets to define the trends for the newcomers—you included!—coming into town. And by and large, those populations are easily classified as "hipster," even if you wouldn't define yourself as a hipster.

I'm still not sure exactly what a hipster is, since it's not exactly spelled out in Detroit media. It's just sort of plopped there as a throwaway term. No local columnist has ever tried to define it, as if it were to be already understood to readers as far as Brownstown Township or Brandon Township what it means.

But it's curious that as media reinforces ideals in their editorial pages about Detroiters coming together, both in the city limits and across county lines, that they continue to beat around a term that's irrationally divisive. I thought that all this time, Detroiters fit into two categories: east side and west side. Chicago does this with north side and south side. New York City does the borough thing.

I'm feeling frustrated, though, because "hipster" is starting to sound like code for something else. We can't put up "whites only" or "colored only" signs anymore up here in the North, but if one were to trace the path of what exactly a hipster is in Detroit, those ancient sentiments feel implied.

For one, we know that hipsters can't be black, since if you do a Google-image search right now of "hipster," you'll find bearded white men in plaid shirts. Here in Detroit, you might drive down Schoolcraft and see bearded black men in plaid shirts. They can't be hipsters, because the dividing line is defined in a 2014 *Huffington Post Detroit* headline: "Detroit doesn't need hipsters, it needs black people." You should read this piece online when you get a chance, because it's actually quite good. But it shows that here in Detroit, blacks aren't hipsters because there's a difference between what black residents bring to the city versus what a "hipster" brings.

So now that we know hipsters in Detroit are indeed white, what does the Detroit hipster wear? Again, it'd always been my general understanding that hipsters wore plaid, at least according to Google images. I also thought hipsters were fans of thrift shops and not wearing designer labels. Not in Detroit. According to the *Detroit Free Press*, hipsters made the rugged Carhartt brand popular outside the construction industry (and not Dr. Dre and Snoop Doggy Dogg two decades ago during the *The Chronic* era, nor the countless hip-hop heads in the years since) and owning a Carhartt jacket is a Detroit hipster staple.

Once we narrow down that hipsters are white people in Carhartts, you might want to ask these hipsters what their purpose is in Detroit. Oftentimes, the media only refers to their role in revitalization. Hipsters, therefore, are incapable of doing bad things: they are not the ones stealing cars in Corktown (that happens if you move there; get a steering wheel lock!), they are not the ones on the City Council asking for raises. They are the superheroes of Detroit, whose methods may irritate the general populace but are inevitably necessary.

Do they have secret hideouts, like the Justice League? No, but you can find them in a handful of bars. WWJ, the news radio station, says the hipsters are at Bronx Bar or PJ's Lager House, which is "hipster heaven." The non-Detroit choices are Whiskey in the Jar in Hamtramck, Gusoline Alley in Royal Oak, and the Loving Touch in Ferndale, which means Macomb County is totally devoid of hipsterism. Anywhere else besides bars? There's a map of spots put together by Bridge, a publication run by a think-tank based in rural Ann Arbor, that says hipsters can only be found—saving?—downtown.

You can also spot a hipster by his—they're clearly not women—haircut. The *Free Press* refined its definition of a Detroit hipster by noting that their hygienic needs are met at "high-end, vintage barbershops" in the Midtown neighborhood.

Doesn't it sound hard to be a hipster in Detroit? I don't think any of these qualifications applied to my late aunt. Hipster or not, however, you should be open-minded enough to not label yourself anyways, and be open-minded enough to know that not just white guys with beards are capable of setting trends. The best way to avoid the hipster trap in Detroit is not to be defined by it.

## THINGS HIPSTERS LIKE, ALLEGEDLY

### URBAN FARMS AND EATING WHOLE

There were a bunch of headlines a few years ago suggesting that urban farming could save Detroit. It hasn't. It has, however, prompted residents to think about what they can do with vacant plots of land. If you're thinking about this, do visit the D-Town Farm over near Rouge Park, operated by the Detroit Black Community Food Security Network, for advice. If you don't want to get your hands dirty and just want to eat good food directly from God's—er, the universe's—green earth, try Goodwells in Midtown, Energy 4 Life Health Food Store on the east side, and, of course, the new Whole Foods in Midtown.

### SHOPPING VINTAGE

You'll find absolutely no shortage of vintage shops and vendors here. Start with Rachel's Place in Corktown, whose owner specifically seeks out American designers and curates collections herself. You'll find vintage wares in Eastern Market on Sundays, too, and also at the huge Salvation Army store outside downtown, Thrift on the Ave in Midtown, and El Dorado General Store in Corktown.

### RECORD STORES

Detroit is home to a number of genres—Motown and other Northern soul, techno, gospel—and that makes digging through the crates an experience. Seriously—people come from across the world just to hang in the record stores here. Try Peoples Records in Eastern Market, Paramita Sound in West Village, Detroit Threads in Hamtramck, almost any flea market in town, and Hello Records in Corktown. Gospel fans should make a point to visit God's World on West Seven Mile Road.

## READING WHAT EVERYONE ELSE ISN'T READING

There is a Barnes & Noble in town, though it is near Wayne State University and not as expansive as larger locations in the region. There are a number of small, indie bookstores, including Source Booksellers in Midtown, Pages Bookshop in Royal Oak, Nandi's Knowledge Café in Highland Park, and Ditto Ditto in Corktown. The granddaddy of bookstores in Detroit, however, is John K. King Books in downtown, one of the largest bookstores in the nation with more than one million volumes.

## GOING TO LITTLE HOLE-IN-THE-WALL PLACES TO SEE SHOWS OR HEAR MUSIC

Cheap, maybe even free, live music is always happening. Pay attention to flyers in bars and restaurants advertising soul nights, house nights, techno nights, folk nights, whatever nights happening at one particular bar on one particular night of the month. Those are impossible to track, so I'm not going to. But a few places where you know you can hear some tunes? Trinosophes, a coffee/art shop in Eastern Market; the Old Miami, a bar (with a lovely outdoor space) in Cass Corridor; PJ's Lager House in Corktown. Fans of Latin music should tour the bars in Southwest Detroit, too.

## LOCAL BEER

OK, fine, if you must. I'm personally of the mindset that beer is beer is beer, but if you're not a PBR-type hipster, your go-to local breweries include Motor City Brewing Works (maker of Ghettoblaster, a top choice among the young and hip), Atwater Brewery, Detroit Beer Co., and Batch Brewing Company. There are plenty more in the region, and know that Bell's Brewery, based way out in Kalamazoo and maker of the ever-popular Oberon, is the statewide favorite. (Short's Brewing Company in Bellaire is a very close second.)

**ARE YOU PROUD TO CALL IT YOUR HOMETOWN?**
*When you come right down to it, I venture to say you'll all agree to*

# A RESOUNDING YES

*when you're talking about*

# DETROIT.

—Smokey Robinson, "I Care About Detroit"

# CHAPTER 20

## HOW TO BE BLACK IN DETROIT

We were late for a school function, so my mother drove a little faster than usual. We were driving to Cornerstone Middle School, which had just opened a new campus on the eastside of Detroit. We were stopped by a police officer.

I don't remember what he said exactly. But I remember what my mother wanted to say, when she was talking with a girlfriend about the incident later. "I wanted to say 'Malice Green,'" she said. The police officer, who was white, berated her for going a few miles over the limit. It wasn't worth his contempt, his condescension. She was let off with a warning, but not let off from the sting of his words.

What could have happened was this: my mother, like Green, a black Detroiter killed by police during a traffic stop in 1992, could have been pulled from the car and beaten to death. Obviously it didn't. But even then, back in 1998—five years after Green's death—it was a very real possibility. Green haunts us, still. Even in this city, where blacks are the majority, your blackness can come under attack.

You're under attack everywhere, it seems. For many of us, discovering and defending your blackness starts in college. We are thrust from our comfortable middle-class brick homes into what we collectively call PWIs—predominately white institutions—in places like East Lansing, Ann Arbor, Mount Pleasant, and Kalamazoo, sharing sardine-can-sized rooms with strangers with preconceived notions.

I started college at Michigan State in 2002, the same year *8 Mile* hit theaters. And I remember having a group discussion in our American Thought and Language class about the film. Our professor, unfamiliar with Detroit, asked if any of us had seen it and whether Detroit was really like the movie. I hadn't yet, but I had remembered sitting in my friend's dorm room, getting super excited seeing Eminem's "Lose Yourself" video for the first time, the elation when we saw the Detroit city skyline in the opening shot. But a white student from the Grosse Pointes had seen it, and gave his opinion.

"It's sort of just like that," I remember him saying. "When you're driving up Jefferson, and cross over the border, you see the change right away."

Detroit and blackness are interwoven; they can't easily be undone. And you are told constantly that you are monolithic, that you are worthless, your existence is incomparable, you had it worse off, you didn't make it out, you did make it out but you're nothing more than an affirmative-action case, you are too defensive, you are loud, dirty, and unkempt, and that you are a malady.

The other Detroit students and I, we corrected our classmate and informed him of where we were from, and told him about those middle-class, brick-house streets far from Eminem's battlegrounds. And that, yes, Eminem did come from a rough part of town but not all of Detroit was "just like that." It's then you realize that white suburban residents have a singular view of what big, black Detroit is, and you will spend the rest of your life defending it.

That was 2002, and I've spent a lot of years since then explaining and explaining to people across the actual Eight Mile that not all of us own guns. I've returned to Detroit stronger, carrying those lessons and always on the defensive, even when I shouldn't be.

But the one thing we didn't count on in college was people like that young Grosse Pointer coming with us to Detroit. If they were made to pay the sins of their parents and grandparents for leaving Detroit for dead, their price was not very high. They simply grew up in a safe if relatively boring suburban environment, and can now afford—thanks to cheaper rent and wide-open spaces—the thrills of the Detroit we've always known.

So, OK. Everybody wants a better Detroit, black, white, whoever. So we fix up our Land Bank homes, and we bury ourselves in laptops at coffeehouse community tables. And we live in harmony, but it's never quite right.

And your blackness comes under attack again. At home.

I sometimes compare being black to pain management of a chronic condition. It is a dull pain, something that can't ever go away but you learn to live with. And then sometimes, beyond your control, the pain flares up and becomes unbearable. There are the dull pains of being black in Detroit, the constant microaggressions. It's when you see a piece in a national publication about Detroit's revival without a single person that looks like you, or when you overhear a New Detroiter commenting about something they just discovered, when it's been there all your life.

When it flares up, it flares up. The police killings in Ferguson and New York City are far from Detroit, but we have had our own share of similar problems. People point directly to Aiyana Stanley-Jones, the seven-year-old girl killed by a Detroit police officer's bullet during a late-night raid. I speak her name, but I always remember Malice Green. A black life in Detroit can fall victim to police brutality, even if the force is more closely reflective of its population than other municipalities.

The killings of Michael Brown and Eric Garner touched me deeply, as they did a lot of us. On the night that a grand jury announced it would not indict Ferguson police officer Darren Wilson for the death of Brown, the pain flared up again. For a lot of us. And the knee-jerk reaction from a *Detroit Free Press* reporter on Twitter was not to empathize with our pain, but to say it didn't exist.

"The lack of a sizable protest tonight in Detroit is another example of the decline of black power here. Even Seattle is having big protests." And that was it. The lack of an indictment in Ferguson was slow. But the unrelated indictment of Detroit's black population from a reporter, if admittedly off the clock, was swift.

And you find yourself defending your blackness again. This time, the lack thereof.

Now, your blackness is under attack because you didn't act fast enough. You didn't provide a non-black person with the reaction they needed to prove your black worth, so now you're feeling less than. Your blackness wasn't enough to pull together a last-minute protest, on one of the coldest days of the year, hours into a dark night to provide a newspaper with a 20-slide photo gallery of grieving black faces holding candles and posters. Your blackness wasn't enough for a one-

or two-day planning session for a proper protest for maximum impact; your blackness demanded immediate action.

And so, a protest was planned. Emails were sent. Announcements were posted on Tumblr, and Facebook, and everywhere else. You texted friends to let them know, put the word out on Twitter, and your blackness was going to be on full display at Noel Night 2014.

I felt the urge to go to Noel Night, a celebration of the holiday season in the city's Midtown area, with my #blacklivesmatter poster, to show that my life did matter, and to defend my blackness yet again. And you would think the critics would be silenced, that even though all the 83% of black Detroit would not be there—maybe because much of the city is without Internet, maybe because there was fear of retribution from the police—there would be enough of us to represent. But then, the new Detroit—the ones that came with us from their suburban enclaves after their parents warned them not to—got upset when you dared to show your blackness.

"Why do they"—*they*—"have to protest here?"

The pendulum shifts. You defend your blackness again because you have to remind the new Detroiters that everything is not peaceful and harmonious for folks like us outside Detroit, and that shit can get real here, too. You are reminded of all the times, again, when you didn't see any black faces in that one article, or why they are trying to rename that one neighborhood where white people are moving in, or why people never want to set foot anywhere near the neighborhoods you grew up in because they say to "stay away from the neighborhoods." The reminder comes again, that blackness and Detroit are interwoven, but now becoming undone because people just want "one Detroit." A "one Detroit" where black people say nothing.

Your blackness is attacked for being on display, and your blackness comes into question when it isn't. I don't remember it ever being this tough to live in Detroit, to be black in Detroit.

So what do you do? White people in Detroit think everything can be solved with conversation. So you bring your blackness to the table, and you still have to play by new rules: be black, but not too black to scare them away, but black enough that they can see you're being black. It makes your head spin and hurt, and you just want to scream and shake their shoulders, but then you'll be called angry and violent.

You don't remember how you got here. The last time you walked into one of the new, trendy bars with your black friends, you drank. Now, the "New Detroit" or the "one Detroit" asks if you had ever drank there in the first place. So now you go to these bars and count the people that look like you, because now your blackness is coming into question among white people who think it doesn't exist because they didn't see it there on opening night. And you can't enjoy your drink.

You just want to get along. Maybe "one Detroit" doesn't sound so bad. The "one Detroit" where we don't talk about blackness. And then the pain will flare up again, because a different group of white people will talk about your blackness for you—in a conversation. Statistics. Observations. Generalizations. You tried to control when your blackness was on display. Now they put your blackness on display for you.

Nothing's ever good enough. And you wonder if it ever will be.

# CLOSING THOUGHTS

Eight Mile is one of Detroit's most famous roads. Perhaps the most famous thanks to the movie. It's fun for people to drive the length of Eight Mile from one end of the city to the other. Maybe even drive farther when the name changes to Base Line Road.

I'd challenge everyone to drive the length of Seven Mile Road instead.

I didn't grow up on Seven Mile, so I can't rep Seven Mile. I do think that driving east to west, or west to east, you can get a fuller scope of what Detroit really is than many other roads.

You see stable neighborhoods off Seven Mile on the west side. You see the destroyed neighborhoods on the east side. You see abandonment on both sides, and beauty on both sides. You see businesses, small and large, on all sides. You see restaurants and bars and grocery stores. You will pass by a golf course, home one of Detroit's remaining leisure activities. You see immigrant enclaves. You see former immigrant enclaves. You see residents that have weathered all the storms. You see schools, churches, community centers.

You'll see cars. You'll see modded cars. Raggedy cars. Brand-new cars. Regular cars.

You'll feel the potholes along the way and they won't be pleasant in the least.

You'll hear passers-by bumping their music as loud as they can.

You cross almost every freeway that chokes this city. You cross north-south thoroughfares that take you to suburbs unknown.

You won't get the full Detroit experience on Seven Mile, because there's no way to get a full Detroit experience in any one sitting. But Seven Mile is as close to quintessential Detroit as it gets. Try it.

And while you're at it: please also try to love this city as much as the rest of us do. That's all we ask.

# ACKNOWLEDGEMENTS

Thank you to my parents, Jill and Bruce, my grandparents, great-grandparents, siblings, aunts, uncles, cousins, play-aunties, play-uncles, play-cousins, and anyone else I consider family for their continued support. I love you all.

Thank you to Keith for making me better, and helping me grow.

Thank you to Motor City Wine and Honest John's in Detroit, The Ugly Mug in Ypsilanti, and several other places with good beverages and/or free wifi for letting me crash your spaces.

Thank you to Matt Hardigree and the good people at *Jalopnik* for letting me rant about Detroit in that sacred car-buff space, and letting this Motor City voice be heard. An additional and heartfelt thanks to the many editors and writers I've worked with and continue to work with over the years—especially the ones that have hired me!

Thank you to Anne Trubek, Martha Bayne, and Belt Publishing for giving me a chance with this project, Haley Stone for the lovely illustrations, and Anna Clark for additional support.

Thanks to anyone who has ever emailed, Facebooked, Tweeted, or handwritten a note of support, no matter how short or long. My peoples from elementary, middle, and high school who have read my musings since the beginning. My *State News* friends for keeping our network of love and support so strong. My MLive and MLive Detroit colleagues who don't get together for drinks as often as we should. The many new friends I've made along the way here in the great city of Detroit. Thank you all for editing, reading, supporting, and criticizing.

# ABOUT THE AUTHOR

Aaron Foley grew up in and currently lives in Detroit, which gives him more street cred than a lot of others. He has written about Detroit for several local and national publications, including *Jalopnik*, CNN, MLive and several others. His essay, "We Love Detroit, Even if You Don't," was included in *A Detroit Anthology* (Belt Publishing, 2014). *How to Live in Detroit Without Being a Jackass* is his first book.